爱的艺术

[古罗马]奥维德 著
戴望舒 译

ARS
AMATORIA

北京联合出版公司
Beijing United Publishing Co.,Ltd.

序 言　驾驭爱的艺术

施蛰存

《爱的艺术》(Ars Amatoria)是古罗马文学史上一部独特的书。它既被斥为坏书,又被誉为天才的著作。作者奥维德的全名是波孛利乌思·奥维提乌思·纳索(Publius Ovidius Naso)。公元前四十三年三月二十日出生于罗马城北九十英里的苏尔莫(Sulmo),现在称为苏尔莫纳。这是现在意大利中部的一个山川清丽、风景幽美的地区。奥维德的父亲是一位富裕的山民,虽然不是贵族,论门第也属于有名望的大家。

幸福的家庭生活,使奥维德没有受到政治、社会动乱的影响。在十二岁的那年，他和比他大一岁的哥哥一起到罗马和雅典去求学。四五年之后,兄弟二人都通过了文法学的考试。十七岁,学成了修辞学,这是罗马青少年教育的最后历程。当时最负盛名的两位学者,亚雷利乌思·傅思古思(Arellius Fuscus)和包尔修·拉脱洛(Porcius Latro),都是奥维德的业师。

按照罗马的制度,一个青年人在完成正规教育以后,必须服兵役一年,然后才可以担任政府公职。但是奥维德没有入伍,他和另一位青年诗人一起去作了一次“壮游”,这是对门第较高的青年的特许,可以通过游学来代替服兵役。他在希腊、西西里岛等处漫游了三年,得到许多浪漫的遭遇和见闻,后来都成为他的诗料。

为了获得一个青年诗人所需要的社交生活和醇酒妇人的享乐，他来到首都罗马。运用他美丽的辞藻和热烈的情感,他写了许多诗篇,呈献给各阶层的美貌女人,从名门闺秀、公主贵妇到歌伶名妓。没过多久,他便声名鹊起,罗马城中所有的女人都对他张臂欢迎。于是他先后写出了《情诗集》《神与巨人的战斗》《女杰传》《妇女美容剂》和《变形记》(有中文译本)

等名篇，深受当时罗马仕女所喜爱，因为这正是罗马的颓废时期，在酣歌恒舞、醇酒妇人的各级社会中，奥维德的诗是投其所好的。

《爱的艺术》全书三卷，第一卷《如何获得爱情》，第二卷《如何保持爱情》，第三卷《女人的良友》。第一、二卷从社会学、心理学基础上对青年男女指导如何处理爱情问题，第三卷专为妇女说法，他提高妇女的社会地位，家庭地位，赞扬妇女的才智并不低于男子，鼓励妇女要更主动地对待爱情生活。这些观点，在当时，事实上是很民主、很进步的，如果不是因为书中有许多色欲的描写，歌颂纵欲的享乐，这三卷诗本来是严肃而纯正的，不至于被视为不道德的淫书。

《爱的艺术》，因为曾经是禁书，因此流传下来的古抄本很少。现在所存，仅牛津、巴黎、维也纳，各有一部。牛津本只有一卷，巴黎本三卷俱全。欧洲几个主要国家的近代译本，都从巴黎本译出。

附录几段欧洲学者对本书的评论，以代本文结束语：

"《爱的艺术》可能是前所未有的最不道德的诗，但并不是最伤风败俗的诗。我们可以怀疑它对读者是否有严重的害处。"(英国马凯尔)

"《爱的艺术》是一本幽默的教育诗，辞藻和内容是非常淫艳的，但它表现了作者对这个问题的渊博的知识和精细的心理学。"(德国史学家杜菲尔和许华勃)

"《爱的艺术》的第一特点是幽默，因为它寓严肃的教育意义于轻浮的内容中……而且它把罗马人的社会生活忠实地记录下来。"(德国向茨)

"奥维德非常讽刺地处理了他的题材。这部诗集完全是讽刺女人的。虽然不如茹汶那尔的《第六讽刺诗》的尖锐刻毒，效果却并不较小。"(英国罗马文学史家渥文)

"《变形记》和《爱的艺术》都是为高度想象力的天才作品，在世界上有重要影响。正如《唐璜》是拜伦的最伟大的作品一样，《爱的艺术》是奥维德最伟大的作品。

"他运用韵律和辞藻的才能已达到了顶峰，他生动、精细的观察力是无可比拟的。"(英国评论家麦考莱)

目 录

CONTENTS

目 录

CONTENTS

FVLIVS OVIDIVS NASO

目　录

CONTENTS

第一卷　如何获得爱情

Book I How to love

I: His Task

Should anyone here not know the art of love, read this, and learn by reading how to love. By art the boat's set gliding, with oar and sail, by art the chariot's swift: love's ruled by art. Automedon was skilled with Achilles's chariot reins, Tiphys in Thessaly was steersman of the Argo, Venus appointed me as guide to gentle Love: I'll be known as Love's Tiphys, and Automedon. It's true Love's wild, and one who often flouts me: but he's a child of tender years, fit to be ruled. Chiron made the young Achilles perfect at the lyre, and tempered his wild spirits through peaceful art. He, who so terrified his enemies and friends, they say he greatly feared the aged Centaur. That hand that Hector was destined to know, was held out, at his master's orders, to be flogged; I am Love's teacher as Chiron was Achilles's, both wild boys, both children of a

1.他的任务

假如在我们的国人中有一个人不懂得爱的艺术，那么他只要读了这部诗作，之后他便能够理解了，他就学会了爱。用帆和桨使船儿航行得很快的是一门艺术，使车儿驰行得很轻捷的也是一门艺术。艺术也能够统治阿谟尔[1]。沃岛美东[2]善于驾车和运用那柔顺的马缰；谛费斯[3]是海木尼阿[4]船的舵工。而我呢，维纳斯[5]曾经叫我做过她的小阿谟尔的老师；人们将称我为阿谟尔的谛费斯和沃岛美东。他生来就非常倔强，他时常与我对抗，但是他还是个孩子，应该是柔顺的年龄，是听人指挥的。菲丽拉[6]的儿子用琴的韵律来教育阿岂赖斯[7]，用这种平寂的艺术，驯服了他的野性。这个人，他曾经多少次让他的同伙和他的敌人感到恐怖，但是有人却说看见他在一个衰颓的老人前退缩颤抖；他的双手使海克笃尔[8]都感到十分有分量，但是当他的老师让他拿出来时，他却会毫不犹豫地伸出来

goddess. Yet the bullock's neck is bowed beneath the yoke, and the spirited horse's teeth worn by the bit. And Love will yield to me, though with his bow he wounds my heart, shakes at me his burning torch. The more he pierces me, the more violently he burns me, so much the fitter am I to avenge the wounds. Nor will I falsely say you gave me the art, Apollo, no voice from a heavenly bird gives me advice, I never caught sight of Clio or Clio's sisterswhile herding the flocks, Ascra, in your

维纳斯的诞生

接受惩罚。岂龙是艾阿古斯[9]的孙子的启蒙老师;我呢,我是阿谟尔的启蒙老师。两个都是让人敬畏的孩子,两个都是女神的儿子[10]。可是骄恣的雄牛终究还是要驾着耕犁的轭,勇敢的战马再剽悍也还是要嚼着那控制着它的辔头。我也是这样,我降伏了阿谟尔,虽然他的箭伤了我的心,而且还在我的面前摇动着他那耀眼的火炬。他的箭越是尖锐,他的火也就越是猛烈,他也就越激起我为了那伤痕而去报复。斐菩斯[11]啊,我决不会冒充说我所教的艺术是受你的影响而来的;传授我这艺术的更不是鸟儿的歌声和羽毛;当我在你的山谷,阿斯克拉[12]牧羊的时候,我没有看见过格丽奥[13]和格丽奥的姊妹们[14],经验是我的导师:听从有心得

valleys: Experience prompts this work: listen to the expert poet. I sing true; Venus, help my venture! Far away from here, you badges of modesty, the thin headband, the ankle-covering dress! I sing of safe love, permissible intrigue, and there'll be nothing sinful in my song.

Now the first task for you who come as a raw recruitis to find out who you might wish to love. The next task is to make sure that she likes you: the third, to see to it that the love will last. That's my aim, that's the ground my chariot will cover: that's the post my thundering wheels will scrape.

的诗人的教诲吧。真实,这就是我要唱的;帮助我吧,阿谟尔,我的母亲!走得远些,你轻盈的细带,贞节的象征[15],而你,曳地的长衣[16],你将我们的贵妇们的纤足遮住了一半!我们要唱的是没有危险的欢乐和得到允许的偷香窃玉[17];我的诗是没有一点可以责备的。

愿意投到维纳斯的旗帜下学习的人,其一,你应当留心去寻找你的恋爱对象;其二,你应当留心去勾引你所爱的女子;其三,要使这爱情维持得久长。这就是我的范围,这就是我的马车要跑的跑道,这就是那应当达到的目的。

Ⅱ: How to Find Her

While you're still free, and can roam on a loose rein, pick one to whom you could say "You alone please me". She won't come falling for you out of thin air: the right girl has to be searched for: use your eyes. The hunter knows where to spread nets for the stag, he knows what valleys hide the angry boar: the wild-fowler knows the woods: the fisherman knows the waters where the most fish spawn: You too, who search for the essence of lasting love, must be taught the places that the girls frequent. I don't demand you set your sails, and search, or wear out some long road to discover them. Perseus brought Andromeda from darkest India, and Trojan Paris snatched his girl from Greece, Rome will grant you lots of such lovely girls, you'll say: "Here's everything the world has had." Your Rome's as many girls as Gargara's sheaves, as Methymna's grapes, as

2.如何找到她

当你的思想一无羁绊，任意驰骋的时候，你可以去选一个女子对她说"只有你才是我最怜爱的人儿"。她是不会乘着一阵舒爽的风儿从天上吹下来的；你最中意的美人是应当用你的眼睛去寻找的。猎人很明白他应该在什么地方张开捕鹿的网，他很清楚在哪一个山谷中有野猪的巢穴。捕鸟的人认识那有利于他捕猎的树林，而渔夫也不会不知道哪一条河中的鱼最多。你也如此，要找一个长久的爱情的目标，也就是首先应该知道在哪里才能够遇到许多少女。要去找她们，你也用不着坐船去航海，也不用到远方去旅行。拜尔塞斯[18]从熏黑的印度人中找到了他的昂德萝美黛[19]，弗里基阿人[20]掠到了一个希腊女子[21]。我很愿意这样。但是单单是一个罗马就已经能够给你一位同样美丽的女子了，而且还如此的多，使你不得不承认，说："我们的城中有世界上最美的人。"正如迦尔迦拉[22]

fishes in the sea, as birds in the hidden branches, stars in the sky: Venus, Aeneas's mother, haunts his city. If you'd catch them very young and not yet grown, real child-brides will come before your eyes: if it's young girls you want, thousands will please you. You'll be forced to be unsure of your desires: if you delight greatly in older wiser years, here too, believe me, there's an even greater crowd.

昂德萝美黛

有丰收的麦穗，麦丁那[23]有盛产的葡萄，海洋里有鱼，树林里有鸟，天上有星一样，在你所居住的罗马，也一样拥有如此众多年轻漂亮的女人。阿谟尔的母亲已在她热爱的艾耐阿斯[24]城中定居了。假如你迷恋那些青春年少又正在发育的美女，一个真正无瑕的少女就会使你感到满意；假如你喜欢年纪大一点的，成千上万的少妇都会使你欢欣，而你便会有选择的困难了。或许一个中年、有经验的妇人在你看来是格外有情趣的。那么，请相信我，这种人是非常多的。

Ⅲ：Search while you're out Walking

Just walk slowly under Pompey's shady colonnade, when the sun's in Leo, on the back of Hercules's lion: or where Octavia added to her dead son Marcellus's gifts, with those rich works of foreign marble. Don't miss the Portico that takes its namefrom Livia its creator, full of old masters: or where the daring Danaids prepare to murder their poor husbands, and their fierce father stands, with out-stretched sword. And don't forget the shrine of Adonis, Venus wept for, and the sacred Sabbath rites of the Syrian Jews. Don't skip the Memphite temple of the linen-clad heifer: she makes many a girl what she herself was to Jove.

And the law-courts (who'd believe it?) they suit love: a flame is often found in the noisy courts: where the Appian waters pulse into the air, from under Venus's temple, made of marble, there the lawyer's often caught

3.在闲逛中寻找

当太阳触到海尔古赖斯的狮子背脊时[25]，你只要到庞培门[26]的阴凉下慢慢地散步，或者是在华丽的纪念物旁漫步，那个建筑物是一位慈母，为了送一件贵重的礼物给她的儿子而让人用异国的云石建造的[27]。不要忘记去欣赏那绘满了古画的廊庑，那里叫丽薇雅[28]，这就是它的创立者；也不要忘记你在那里可以看见那些谋害不幸的堂兄弟们的培鲁斯的孙女们[29]，和她们手中握着剑的残忍的父亲[30]的轮廓[31]。更不要忘记维纳斯为之哀哭的阿陶尼斯[32]节，和叙利亚的犹太人每个礼拜的第七日所举行的大祭典。更不要避开牝牛，埃及的披着麻衣的女神的神殿；她使许多妇人都模仿她对裘比德做的事[33]。

即使那市场（谁会相信呢？）也是有利于阿谟尔的，不管它有多少喧闹，一缕感情的火焰还是会从那里生出来。在供奉着维纳斯的云石的神

by love, and he who guides others, fails to guide himself: in that place of eloquence often his words desert him, and a new case starts, his own cause is the brief. There Venus, from her neighbouring temples, laughs: he, who was once the counsel, now wants to be the client.

奥格斯特的妻子丽薇雅

殿下,阿比阿斯[34]用飞泉射到空中。在那个地方,有许多法学家被阿谟尔所绑缚,而这些能保护别人的人却不能保护自己。经常地,在这个地方,即使最善辩的人也缺乏辞令:新的利益占据着他,使他不得不为自己的利害进行辩论。在邻近的地方,维纳斯在她的神殿里微笑着看他的窘态;在不久之前还是保护别人的人,现在却只希望受到别人的保护了。

Ⅳ：At the Theatre

But hunt for them，especially，at the tiered theatre：that place is the most fruitful for your needs. There you'll find one to love，or one you can play with，one to be with just once，or one you might wish to keep. As ants return home often in long processions，carrying their favourite food in their mouths，or as the bees buzz through the flowers and thyme，among their pastures and fragrant chosen meadows，so our fashionable ladies crowd to the famous shows：my choice is often constrained by such richness. They come to see，they come to be seen as well：the place is fatal to chaste modesty. These shows were first made troublesome by Romulus，when the raped Sabines delighted unmarried men. Then no awnings hung from the marble theatre，the stage wasn't stained with saffron perfumes：Then what the shady Palatine provided，leaves simply

4.在剧院里

你尤其应该在剧院和它的半圆形的座位中撒开你的网：这些地方都充满了机会。在那里，你可以找到某个能够打动你、某个你可以欺骗、某个不过是路边的闲花野草、某个你可以和她建立长久关系的人。好像蚂蚁在长阵中来来往往地运输着它们的食品谷子，或者像那些蜜蜂找到了它们所喜爱的香草时，轻轻地在茄香和花枝上飞舞。女子也是如此，穿着艳丽的服饰，忙着向剧院蜂拥而去；她们的数目往往使我在选择的时候感到非常为难。她们是去看戏的，可是她们同时也是去被看的，这对于贞洁来说是一个非常危险的地方。这就是你的开端啊，罗摩路斯[35]！你将烦恼混到了游艺之中，掳掠沙皮尼族[36]的女子给你的战士做妻子。那时剧院的垂幕还没有装饰云石，番红花汁还没有染红舞台。从巴拉丁山的树上采下来的树叶的彩带是并不精致的剧场的唯一装饰品。在分做层级的

placed, was all the artless scene. The audience sat on tiers made from turf, and covered their shaggy hair, as best they could, with leaves. They watched, and each with his eye observed the girl he wanted, and trembled greatly in his silent heart. While, to the measure of the homely Etruscan flute, the dancer, with triple beat, struck the levelled earth, amongst the applause (applause that was never artful then) the king gave the watched-for signal for the rape. They sprang up straightaway, showing their intent by shouting, and eagerly took possession of the women. As doves flee the eagle, in a frightened crowd, as the new-born lamb runs from the hostile wolf: so they fled in panic from the lawless men, and not one showed

罗马的建设者罗摩路斯

草地的座位上，人民都坐着，树叶漫过了他们的头发。每个人都向自己的周围观望，搜寻他所渴望的少女，在心中悄悄地做着自己的打算。当号角声响起，一个狂剧的演员用脚在平地上顿了三下，在人民的欢呼声中，罗摩路斯发出暗号给他的部下，让他们夺取各人的猎物。他们突然发出那泄露他们阴谋的呼声向前奔去，用他们贪婪的手扑向年轻的处女。正如一群受到惊吓的小鸽子在老鹰的前面飞翔，正如一头小绵羊看到狼的影子而拼命奔逃，沙皮尼的女子也一样颤抖着，当她们看见那些蛮横的战士向她们扑过来时。她们全都脸色

the colour she had before. Now they all fear as one, but not with one face of fear. Some tear their hair; some sit there, all will lost; one mourns silently, another cries for her mother in vain; one moans, one faints; one stays, while that one runs; the captive girls were led away, a joyful prize, and many made even fear itself look fitting. Whoever showed too much fight, and denied her lover, he held her clasped high to his loving heart, and said to her "Why mar your tender cheeks with tears? As your father to your mother, I'll be to you." Romulus, alone, knew what was fitting for soldiers: I'll be a soldier, if you give me what suits me. From that I suppose came the theatres' usual customs: now too they remain a snare for the beautiful.

惨白:因为她们都很惊慌,虽然惊慌的表现各不相同。有的是自己抓着自己的头发,有的则是坐在自己的位置上晕过去了;这个默默地哭泣,那个徒然地喊着她的母亲;其余的或者是呜咽着,或者是被惊呆了;有的则一动不动地站着,有的想要逃走。人们便牵着那些女子——注定是他们婚床上的猎物,有许多女子因为惊慌而显得格外美丽。假如有一个女子剧烈反抗,不肯顺从那个想要抢她的人,那么那人便抱起她,热情地将她紧贴在胸口,对她说:"为什么要用眼泪来破坏你那美丽眼眸的光辉呢?你父亲是如何对待你母亲的,我就会如何来对待你。"哦,罗摩路斯!只有你能适当地奖赏你的士兵:为了这种奖品,我很愿意投到你的旗帜之下。这是一定的,由于对这古老习惯的效忠,直到现在,剧场里还为美人们设着陷阱。

Ⅴ:At the Races，or the Circus

Don't forget the races，those noble stallions: the Circus holds room for a vast obliging crowd. No need here for fingers to give secret messages，nor a nod of the head to tell you she accepts: you can sit by your lady; nothing's forbidden，press your thigh to hers，as you can do，all the time; and it's good the rows force you close，even if you don't like it，since the girl is touched through the rules of the place. Now find your reason for friendly conversation，and first of all engage in casual talk. Make earnest enquiry whose those horses are: and rush to back her favourite，whatever it is. When the crowded procession of ivory gods goes by，you clap fervently for Lady Venus: if by chance a speck of dust falls in the girl's lap，as it may，let it be flicked away by your fingers: and if there's nothing，flick away the nothing: let anything be a reason for you to serve

5.在跑马场，或竞技场

更不要忘了那骏马竞赛的跑马场。这个聚集着无数群众的竞技场，也是有很多机会的。用不着做手势来掩饰你的秘密，而点头也是不需要的，不需要借助这些来表示你的一种特殊作用。你去坐在她的身旁，并排地坐着，越贴近越好，这是不会有什么妨碍的：狭窄的位子使她和你挤得很紧，她是没有办法的，而你却是幸福极了。于是你便找一个话题和她谈话，起初先和她说几句普通的话题，当骏马进入竞技场的时候：你便急忙去问她马的主人的名字，随便她喜欢哪一匹马，你就要立刻附和她。可是，当那以壮士相斗作为先导的赛神会的长列进来的时候[37]，你便兴高采烈地对她的保护人维纳斯喝彩。假如，偶然有一点尘埃飞到你的美人儿的胸口，你要轻轻地用手指拂去它；假如没有尘埃，你也尽可以去拂拭着：总之你应当去用那些冠冕堂皇的理由。她的衣裙是曳在地上的吗？你

her. If her skirt is trailing too near the ground, lift it, and raise it carefully from the dusty earth. Straightaway, the prize for service, if she allows it, is that your eyes catch a glimpse of her legs. Don't forget to look at who's sitting behind you, that he doesn't press her sweet back with his knee. Small things please light minds: it's very helpful to puff up her cushion with a dextrous touch. And it's good to raise a breeze with a light fan, and set a hollow stool beneath her tender feet. And the Circus brings assistance to new love, and the scattered sand of the gladiator's ring. Venus' boy often fights in that sand, and who see wounds, them selves receive a wound. While talking, touching hands, checking the programme, and

爱的保护神维纳斯

要将它揭起来，使得没有什么东西可以弄脏它。因为你的这种殷勤，她一点也不会恼怒，反而会给你一个瞻仰她美腿的恩惠作为回报。此外你更应当注意坐在她后面的看客，恐怕那伸得太长的膝踝会碰到她的肩头。这些琐细的事情都能笼络住她们轻盈的灵魂：多少多情的男子在一个美女的身边获得成功，就是因为他小心地安好一个坐垫，用一把扇子为她摇风，或是放一张踏脚凳在她的纤足下。这些都是获得新爱情的好机会，你都可以在竞技场和因为结怨的烦躁所变作忧愁的市场中找到。阿谟尔时常欢喜在那儿作战，在那里，是看着别人伤痕的人，自己却感到受了伤；他说话，他为这个或者那个参加相扑的人而和人打赌，他刚接触到对方

asking, having bet, which one will win, wounded he groans, and feels the winged dart, and himself becomes a part of the show he sees.

When, lately, Caesar, in mock naval battle, exhibited the Greek and Persian fleets, surely young men and girls came from either coast, and all the peoples of the world were in the City? Who did not find one he might love in that crowd? Ah, how many were tortured by an alien love!

恺撒大帝

的手,他就会摆出东道主的架势问谁获胜了。忽然一支飞快的箭穿透了他,他惨叫一声。于是起初只是看角斗的看客而已,如今自己却变成了牺牲者之一。

不久之前,恺撒[38]让我们看关于海战的戏,在那里,波斯的战舰和凯克洛泊斯的儿郎[39]的战舰交战[40],那时青年男女都从各处跑来看这场戏:罗马在那时好像是一个世界的幽会地。在这人群中,谁没有找到一个恋爱的目的物呢?啊!多少人都被一缕异国的情焰烧得焦头烂额!

Ⅵ：Triumphs are Good too！

Behold，now Caesar's planning to add to our rule what's left of earth：now the far East will be ours. Parthia，we'll have vengeance：Crassus's bust will cheer，and those standards wickedly laid low by barbarians. The avenger's here，the leader，proclaimed，of tender years，and a boy wages war's un-boy-like agenda. Cowards，don't count the birthdays of the gods：a Caesar's courage flowers before its time. Divine genius grows faster than its years，and suffers as harmful evils the cowardly delays. Hercules was a child when he crushed two serpentsin both his hands，already worthy of Jupiter in his cradle. How old were you，Bacchus，who are still a boy，when conquered India trembled to your rod? Your father's years and powers arm you，boy，and with your father's powers and years you'll win：though your first beginnings must be in debt

6.美好的胜利

可是恺撒准备去统一全世界了。现在，遥远的东方啊，你们将属于我们了！巴尔底人[41]啊，你们就要受到惩罚了！克拉苏斯[42]，在你的墓中尽情享乐吧；而你们，不幸落在蛮族手中的旗帜啊，你们的复仇者已经前进了！年纪还很轻的时候，他就具有英雄的气概，虽然还是个孩子[43]，他却已经指挥那孩子进入他的力量还无法达到的军队了。怯懦的人们，不要去计算神祇的年龄吧：恺撒们的勇敢是超过他们年龄的。他们的神明的天才因为走在时间的前面而发怒，不能忍耐缓慢的成长。还是一个小小的婴儿，谛伦斯的英雄[44]已经用他的手扼死了两条蛇：他从小就做裘比德的孩子了。而你，总是一副儿童模样的巴古斯[45]，你是多么伟大啊，当战败的印度在你的松球杖[46]前战栗时！孩子啊[47]！在你祖先的保护之下用

to such a name, now prince of the young, but one day prince of the old: Your brothers are with you, avenge your brothers' wounds: your father is with you, keep your father's laws. Your and your country's father endowed you with arms: the enemy stole his kingship from an unwilling parent: You hold a pious shaft, he a wicked arrow: Justice and piety stick to your standard. Let Parthia's cause be lost: and their armies: let my leader add Eastern wealth to Latium. Both your fathers, Mars and Caesar, grant you power: through you one is a god, and one will be. See, I augur your triumph: I'll reply with a votive song, and you'll be greatly celebrated on

罗马大将克拉苏斯

你祖先的勇气战胜他人：只有这样的一个开端才能与你的盛名相符。今天的青年王侯，有一天你将会成为元老院的议长。你有许多兄弟，要为你兄弟们所受的那些侮辱报仇啊！你有一个父亲，拥护你父亲的权力啊！交付你兵权的是国父，也是你自己的父亲；只有仇敌，他才会篡夺父亲的王位[48]。你呢，佩带着神圣的武器；他呢，佩带着箭。人们会看见，在你的旗帜前面，神圣的正义正在前进。本来是屈于理的，他们当然也就屈于兵力了！愿我的英雄将东方的财富带到拉丁姆[49]来。马尔斯神[50]，还有你，恺撒神，在他出发的时候，助他一臂神力吧，因为你们两个中的一个已经成为神了，另一个有朝一日也将成为神。是的，我已经预测到了，你将战胜的，我许下一个心愿为你作一首诗，在那里我的嘴能够为你找到

my lips. You'll stand and exhort your troops with my words: Oh let my words not lack your courage! I'll speak of Parthian backs and Roman fronts, and shafts the enemy hurl from flying horses. If you flee, to win, Parthia, what's left for you in defeat? Mars already has your evil eye. So the day will be, when you, beautiful one, golden, will go by, drawn by

酒神巴古斯

流利的音调。我将你描写成全身披挂的勇士,用一篇关于理想的演说鼓励你的士卒。我希望我的诗能够配得上你的英武!我将描写巴尔底人转身逃走,而罗马人则奋起直追,敌人在逃跑时从马上发出箭来。哦,巴尔底人,你想全师而退,可是你战败后还剩下些什么呢?巴尔底人啊,从此

four snowy horses. The generals will go before you，necks weighed down with chains，lest they flee to safety as they did before. The happy crowd of youths and girls will watch，that day will gladden every heart. And if she，among them，asks the name of a king，what place，what mountains，and what stream's displayed，you can reply to all，and more if she asks：and what you don't know，reply as memory prompts. That's Euphrates，his brow crowned with reeds：that'll be Tigris with the long green hair. I make those Armenians，that's Persia's Danaan crown：that was a town in the hills of Achaemenia. Him and him，they're generals：and say what names they have，if you can，the true ones，if not the most fitting.

以后马尔斯只给你一个不祥的预兆。世人中的最美者，有一天我们将会看见你满披着黄金[51]，驾着四匹白马回到我们的城下。在你的前面，走着那些颈上系着铁链的敌军将领们：他们已经不能像从前那样逃走了。青年和少女都将快乐地参与这个盛会，这一天将是大快人心的；那时假如有一个少女问你那些人身上背着的画图上的战败王侯的名字，还有就是那些地方、那些河流，你应当完完全全地回答她，而且不要等她问起才告诉她；即使有些是你所不知道的，你也要当做好像很熟悉的样子说出来。这就是幼发拉底河[52]，那额上缠着芦苇的，那披着深蓝色假发的，就是底格里斯河；那些走过来的，说他们是亚美尼亚[53]人，这个女子就是波斯，她的第一个国王就是达纳爱[54]的儿子；这是一座在阿凯曼耐斯子孙[55]的山谷中的城市。这个囚徒或者那个囚徒都是将士；假如你能够，你便可以照着他们的脸儿取名字，至少要和他们相合。

Ⅶ: There's always the Dinner-Table

The table laid for a feast also gives you an opening: there's something more than wine you can look for there. Often rosy Love has clasped Bacchus's horns, drawing him to his gentle arms, as he lay there. And when wine has soaked Cupid's drunken wings, he's stayed, weighed down, a captive of the place. It's true he quickly shakes out his damp feathers: though still the heart that's sprinkled by love is hurt. Wine rouses courage and is fit for passion: care flies, and deep drinking dilutes it. Then laughter comes, the poor man dons the horns, then pain and sorrow leave, and wrinkled brows. Then what's rarest in our age appears to our minds, Simplicity: all art dispelled by the god. Often at that time girls captivated men's wits, and Venus was in the vine, flame in the fire. Don't trust the treacherous lamplight overmuch: night and wine can harm your

7.永恒的晚宴

筵席和宴会中也有绝好的机会,人们在那里所找到的不只是饮酒的欢乐。在那里,红色脸颊的阿谟尔将巴古斯的两个侍从拥在他纤细的臂间。等到他的翅膀被酒浸湿时,沉重得不能飞翔的柯毗陀便一动不动地停留在原处了。可是不久他便又摇动起他那湿漉漉的翅膀,于是那些心上沾着这种炎热露水的人便遭遇不幸了。酒将心安置在温柔中使它易于燃烧;烦虑全消失了,被狂饮所消耗了。于是欢笑来了;于是穷人也鼓起了勇气,相信自己是富人了:更没有痛苦、不安;额上的皱纹也平复下去了,心花怒放,而在今天则是如此罕见的爽直把矫饰驱逐了。在那里,青年人的心是经常被少女所束缚住的:酒后的维纳斯,更是火上加火。可是你千万不要轻信那欺人的灯光:为了评判美人,夜和酒都不是好的评判者。那是在白天,在阳光之下,巴黎斯看见那三位女神[56],对维纳斯说:

view of beauty. Paris saw the goddesses in the light, a cloudless heaven, when he said to Venus: "Venus, you win, over them both." Faults are hidden at night: every blemish is forgiven, and the hour makes whichever girl you like beautiful. Judge jewellery, and fabric stained with purple, judge a face, or a figure, in the light.

神界三女神

"你胜过你的两个敌人,维纳斯。"黑夜抹杀了许多污点又隐藏了许多缺陷:在那个时候,任何女人都似乎是美丽的。人们评判宝石和红绫是在白天,所以评判人体的线条和容貌也必须在白天。

Ⅷ: And Finally There's the Beach

Why enumerate every female meeting place fit for the hunter? The grains of sand give way before the number. Why speak of Baiae, its shore splendid with sails, where the waters steam with sulphurous heat? Here one returning, his heart wounded, said: "That water's not as healthy as they claim." Behold the suburban woodland temple of Diana, and the kingdom murder rules with guilty hand. She, who is virgin, who hates Cupid's darts, gives people many wounds, has many to give.

月神第阿娜

8.最终的海岸

我难道要计算能够猎取美人的一切地点吗?我还不如去计算海沙的数目。我要说的是拔页[57],拔页的沿岸和那滚着浓烟的硫黄泉浴池。在出浴的时候,许许多多洗浴人的心灵都受到了创伤,又喊着:"这受人称颂的水并没有像别人所说的那样达到卫生的标准。"在离罗马城不远的地方,便是第阿娜[58]的神殿,那里树木成荫,这个主权是用鲜血和干戈换来的。因为她是处女,因为她害怕柯毗陀的箭,这女神已经伤害了她的许多信徒,以后还将会伤到许多。

Ⅸ: How To Win Her

So far, riding her unequal wheels, the Muse has taught you where you might choose your love, where to set your nets. Now I'll undertake to tell you what pleases her, by what arts she's caught, itself a work of highest art. Whoever you are, lovers everywhere, attend, with humble minds, and you, masses, show you support me: use your thumbs.

First let faith enter into your mind: every one of them can be won; you'll win her, if you only set your snares. Birds will sooner be silent in the Spring, cicadas in summer, an Arcadian hound turn his back on a hare, than a woman refuse a young man's flattering words: even she you might think dislikes it, will like it. Secret love's just as pleasing to women as men. Men pretend badly: she hides her desire. If it was proper for men not to be the first to ask, woman's role would be to take the part of the

9.如何赢得她

在哪里选择你爱情的目标?在哪里布下你的网?到现在,坐在一辆车轮不平衡的车上的达丽阿[59]已经给你指示了。如今我所要教你的是如何去笼络住你所爱的人儿;我的功课最要紧的地方就在这里。各地的多情人,希望你们能够听从我的话,愿我的演说能够找到一个场地。

第一,你必须坚信任何女子都可以得到:你将得到她们;你尽管布你的网就是了。假如女子会不接受男子的挑拨,那么就如同春天没有鸟儿的歌声,夏天就没有蝉的高唱,野兔子能够赶跑梅拿鲁思[60]的狗。你以为她是不愿意的,其实她心中早已暗暗地愿意了。偷偷摸摸的恋爱在女子看来是和男子的观点一样的,即别有风味的:但是男子不知道矫作,而女子却将她们的心情掩饰得很好。假如男子都不先出手,那已经屈服的女子立刻就会出手了。在芳草地上,牝牛多情地呼叫着雄牛;牝马在靠近雄马时则

asker. The cow lows to the bull in gentle pastures: the mare whinnies to the hoofed stallion. Desire in us is milder and less frantic: the male fire has its lawful limits. Remember Byblis, who burned with incestuous love, for her brother, and bravely punished herself with the noose? Myrrha loved her father, but not as a daughter should, and then was hidden by the covering bark: oozing those tears, that pour from the tree as fragrance, and whose droplets take their name from the girl. Once, in the shady valleys of wooded Ida there was a white bull, glory of the herd, one small black mark set between his horns: it the sole blemish, the rest was milky-

岂尼拉斯的女儿米拉

不断嘶鸣。在我们人类中,热情是格外受到节制的,而不是奔放的:人类的情焰是不会和自然之理相违背的。我要说皮勃丽思吗?她为了她的哥哥燃起了罪恶的情焰,然后自缢了,勇敢地去责罚自己的罪恶[61]。米拉[62]爱她的父亲,可是并不是用一种女儿对父亲的爱情;如今她已将她的羞耻隐藏在那裹住她的树皮中了,成了芳树,她流淌出来的眼泪成为我们的香料,也保留下了这不幸女子的名字。在长满了灌木丛的伊达[63]幽谷中,有一头白色的雄牛,这是牛群的光荣。它的额头上有一点小黑斑,只有这一点,是在两角之间;身上其余的地方完全是乳白色的。格洛苏思[64]和启道

white. The heifers of Cnossos and Cydon longed to have him mount up on their backs. Pasiphae joyed in adultery with the bull: she hated the handsome heifers with jealousy. I sing what is well-known: not even Crete, the hundred-citied, can deny it, however much Cretans lie. They say that, with unpractised hands, she plucked fresh leaves and tenderest grasses for the bull. She went as one of the herd, unhindered by any carefor that husband of hers: Minos was ousted by a bull. Why put on your finest clothes, Pasiphae? Your lover can appreciate none of your wealth. Why have a mirror with you, when you seek highland cattle? Why

克来特之王米诺思

奈阿[65]的牝牛都争相以被它压在身下为荣。葩西法艾[66]渴望做它的情妇；她妒恨着那些美丽的牝牛。这是一个已经得到证实的事情；那坐拥百城的克来特[67]，专门说谎欺骗别人的克来特，也不能否认这个事实。别人说葩西法艾，用那不熟练的手，亲自采摘鲜叶和嫩草给雄牛吃，而且，为了能够陪伴它，她连自己的丈夫都忘记了：一头雄牛，竟胜于米诺思[68]。葩西法艾，你为什么穿着这样豪华的衣服？你的情夫是不懂你的富丽的。当你到山上去与牛群约会时，为什么要拿着一面镜子？你为什么不停地理

continually smooth your hair, you foolish woman? But believe the mirror that denies you're a heifer. How you wish that brow of yours could bear horns! If you'd please Minos, don't seek out adulterers: If you want to cheat your husband, cheat with a man! The queen left her marriage bed for woods and fields, like a Maenad roused by the Boeotian god, they say. Ah, how often, with angry face, she spied a cow, and said: "Now, how can she please my lord? Look, how she frisks before him in the tender grass: doubtless the foolish thing thinks that she's lovely." She spoke, and straightaway had her led from the vast herd, the innocent thing dragged under the arching yoke, or felled before the altar, forced to be a false sacrifice, and, delighted, held her rival's entrails in her hand. The number of times she killed rivals to please the gods, and said, holding the entrails: "Go, and please him for me!" Now she claims to be Io, and now Europa, one who's a heifer, the other borne by the bull. Yet he filled her, the king of the herd, deceivedby a wooden cow, and their offspring

着你的发丝？多么愚笨！至少应该相信你的镜子吧：它会告诉你，你不是一头母牛。你是多么希望在你的额上长出两只角来啊！假如你是爱米诺思的，那么就不要去找情夫了吧，或者，假如你要欺骗你的丈夫，至少也要和一个"人"通奸啊！可是偏偏不是如此，那王后遗弃了龙床，奔波于树林之间，像一个被阿沃尼阿的神祇[69]所激动的跳神女人[70]一样。多少次，她把那妒忌的目光投在一头母牛的身上，说："它为什么会得到我心上人的欢心？你看它在它前面的草地上多么欢跃啊！这蠢货无疑是自以为这样可以显得更可爱了。"她说着便立刻吩咐将那头母牛从牛群中牵出来，或是使它把头低在轭下，或者是使它倒毙在一个没有诚心的献祀的祭坛下；于是她充满了欢乐将她情敌的心脏拿在手中。她多次杀戮她的情敌，假装说是去熄灭神祇的怒火，又拿着它们的心脏说："现在你去取悦我的情郎吧！"有时她愿意做欧罗巴[71]，有时她羡慕伊沃[72]的命运：因为一个是母牛，还有一个是被一头雄牛驮在背上的。可是被一头木头做的母牛像所蛊惑，那牛群的王让葩西法艾怀了孕，而她所产出来的果子[73]却泄露

betrayed its breeding. If Cretan Aerope had spurned Thyestes's love (and isn't it hard to forego even one man?), the Sun would not have veered from his course mid-way, and turned back his chariot and horses towards Dawn. The daughter who savaged Nisus's purple lockpresses rabid dogs down with her thighs and groin. Agamemnon who escaped Mars on land, Neptune at sea, became the victim of his murderous wife. Who would not

谛爱斯带思

出她的耻辱。假如另一个克来特女子[74]不去爱谛爱斯带思[75](妇人专一地爱着一个男子是一桩多么难的事情啊),人们不会看见斐菩斯在他的路上停止,回转他的车子,驾着他的马奔向东方。尼须思的女儿[76],为了割下她父亲光辉的头发,变成了一个腰围上长着许多恶狗的怪物。阿特拉思的儿子[77]在地上脱逃了马尔斯,在海上脱逃了奈泊都诺思[78],但终究不幸成为了他妻子的牺牲者。谁不曾将眼泪洒在那烧着爱弗拉[79]的克莱乌莎[80]的情焰上,和在那染着血的杀了自己孩子的母亲身上[81]?阿明托尔的儿子斐尼克思[82]因为失去他的眼睛而痛哭。伊包里度思[83]的骏马,在你们的惊恐中,将你们主人的身体弄碎了!弗纳思[84],你为什么要挖去你无辜的孩子们的眼睛啊?报应将会重复落在你的头上。妇人中无羁的热情和放荡是这样的:比我们的还要热烈,还要奔放。勇敢啊,带着一颗必胜的

weep at Corinthian Creusa's flames, and that mother bloodstained by her children's murder? Phoenix, Amyntor's son wept out of sightless eyes: Hippolytus was torn by his fear-maddened horses. Phineus, why blind your innocent sons? That punishment will return on your own head. All these things were driven by woman's lust: it's more fierce than ours, and more frenzied. So, on, and never hesitate in hoping for any woman: there's hardly one among them who'll deny you. Whether they give or not, they're delighted to be asked: And even if you fail, you'll escape unharmed. But why fail, when there's pleasure in new delightsand the more foreign the more they capture the heart? The seed's often more fertile in foreign fields, and a neighbour's herd always has richer milk.

尼须思的女儿

信心上阵;在一千个女子中,能抵抗你的连一个都找不到。她们接纳也好,拒绝也罢,她们总是喜欢别人去献好的;即使你被拒绝了,这种失败对于你来说是没有任何危险的。可是你怎么会被拒绝呢?一个人经常会在新的陶醉中找到欢乐:别人的东西总是比自己的好。总觉得别人田地中的收获格外丰饶,邻居家的牲畜总是格外肥壮。

X: First Secure the Maid

But to get to know your desired-one's maidis your first care: she'll smooth your way. See if she's close to her mistress's thoughts, and has plenty of true knowledge of her secret jests. Corrupt her with promises, and with prayers: you'll easily get what you want, if she wishes. She'll tell the time (the doctors would know it too) when her mistress's mind is receptive, fit for love. Her mind will be fit for love when she luxuriatesin fertility, like the crop on some rich soil. When hearts are glad, and nothing sad constrains them, they're open: Venus steals in then with seductive art. So Troy was defended with sorrowful conflict: in joy, the Horse, pregnant with soldiers, was received. She's also to be tried when she's wounded, pained by a rival: make it your task then to see that she's avenged. The maid can rouse her, when she combs her hair in the morning, and add her

10.先从女佣着手

你首先要先结识你所逢迎的女子的侍女:因为能够为你进门提供方便的就是她。先要确信,她的女主人是否完全信任她,她是否是她女主人秘密和欢乐的忠诚的同谋者。为了要得到她,许愿和央求一件也少不了;这样你所要求的,她都会为你办到;一切都是出于她的高兴。她会选择一个恰当的时候(医生也是注意时候的);要趁她女主人容易说话的时候,最受勾引的时候。在那个时候,一切都向她微笑着,欢乐在她的眼中发着光,正如金穗在丰收的田野中一样。当心怀欢乐的时候,当它不为忧苦所束缚的时候,它便自然地开放了;那时维纳斯便轻轻地溜了进去。伊里雍正陷入愁困中,他的军队正和希腊的军队相对抗;而迎接藏着战士的木马进城那天,却是一个快乐的日子啊[85]!你更要选她受到对手侮辱而啜泣的时候,使她可以让你做她的报复者。早晨,正在理发的时候,侍女触

oar to the work of your sails, and sighing to herself in a low murmur, say: "But I doubt that you'll be able to make her pay." Then she should speak of you, and add persuasive words, and swear you're dying, crazed with love. But hurry, lest the sails fall and the breeze dies: anger melts away, with time, like fragile ice. You ask perhaps if one should take the maid herself? Such a plan brings the greatest risk with it. In one case, fresh from bed, she'll get busy, in another be tardy, in one case you're a prize for her mistress, in the other herself. There's chance in it: even if it favours the idea, my advice nevertheless is to abstain. I don't pick my way over sharp peaks and precipices, no youth will be caught out being lead by me. Still, while she's giving and taking messages, if her body pleases

维纳斯出浴

怒了她。为了你,她借此机会张帆打桨,低声地说,还一边叹息着:"我不相信你能够恩怨分明。"于是她便说起了你,她为你说了一番动心的话,她说你将为情而死。可是你应当迅速行动,不然风就要停了,帆就要落了。怒气就像薄冰一样,一会儿就会融化的。你也许要问我了:先得到那侍女的欢心有什么用吗?这种办法是很偶然的。有的侍女用这种办法果然能够使她格外热心地为你出力,有的反而不热心了:这个为你照料她的女主人,那个却将你留下自己受用了。大胆的人获得了

you as much as her zeal, make the lady your first priority, her companion the next: love should never be begun with a servant. I warn you of this, if art's skill is to be believed, and don't let the wind blow my words out to sea; follow the thing through or don't attempt it; she'll endure the whispers once she's guilty herself. It's no help if the bird escapes when its wings are limed: it's no good if the boar gets free from a loosened net. Hold fast to the stricken fish you've caught on the hook: press home the attempt, don't leave off till you've won. She'll not give you away, sharing the guilt for the crime, and you'll know whatever your lady's done, and said. But hide it well: if the informer's well hidden, you'll always secretly know your mistress's mind.

成功,即使这句话能够助长你的勇气,按照我的意见:还是慎重些好。因为我是不会到悬崖绝壁上找我的路的;让我来做引导的人,是不会走入迷途的。可是当侍女传递书简的时候,她的美丽和热情不次于她的热忱,你必须以得到那女主人为先,侍女自然随后也就来了;可是你的爱却不应该从她开始。只有一个劝告,假如你对于我所教的功课有几分信心,假如我的话没有被狂风吹到大海去,千万不要冒险,否则就会彻底失败。一旦这件风流案侍女有了一半的份儿,她便不会背叛你了。翅膀上沾着黍胶的鸟是不能远飞的;野猪在笼住它的网中挣扎是徒劳的;鱼一旦上了钩,就不能逃脱。你已经挑逗了的,你必须快快紧逼,一直到胜利后才放手。可是你要瞒得好好的!假如侍女将你的聪敏隐藏得很好,你的情妇所做的一切对你来说也就没有什么神秘的了。

Ⅺ: Don't Forget Her Birthday!

It's a mistake to think that only farmers working the fields, and sailors, need to keep an eye on the season: seed can't always be trusted to the furrow, or a hollow ship to the wine-dark sea, it's not always safe to capture tender girls; Often the time itself makes for success. If her birthday's here, or the April Kalends, that delight in joining months, Venus's to Mars, or if the Circus is decorated, not as beforewith clay figurines but with the wealth of kings, delay the thing: then winter's harsh, the Pleiades are here, then the tender Kid is merged with the ocean wave; it's best to hold off then; then he who trusts the deep, can scarcely save the wreckage of his mangled boat. It's fine to start on that day of tears when the Allia flowed with the blood poured from Roman wounds, or when the Sabbath day returns, the holy day of the Syrian Jews, less suitable for

11.千万不要忘记她的生日!

相信只有农夫和水手才应当顾虑时间,这实在是一个大错误。正如不应该一年到头在那一块会欺骗我们的土地上播种一样,或者是不时地将一只小舟放到碧海上去一般,一天到晚地向一个美人进攻也是靠不住的。等着一个好机会,人们时常能够很好地达到目的。假如你在她的生日或者历书上紧接着维纳斯喜欢的爱人马尔斯的日子[86],当竞技场已不像从前那样装饰着小雕像,而是陈设着从失败者那得到的战利品时,你就要停止了;于是凄惨的冬天来了,于是百莱阿代恩[87]近了,于是温柔的山羊沉到大海中去了[88]。那便是休息的好时候,谁要是不自量力地到海上去,那么他的船就会被击得粉碎,甚至连性命都难保。着手于那使人流很多眼泪的,拉丁族的血染红了阿里阿河[89]的日子,或者是在巴莱斯底那的叙利亚人每周所庆祝的安息日。你要十分留意你密友的生日,你更要

buying things. Let your mistress's birthday be one of great terror to you: that's a black day when anything has to be given. However much you avoid it, she'll still win: it'sa woman's skill, to strip wealth from an ardent lover. A loose-robed pedlar comes to your lady: she likes to buy; and explains his prices while you're sitting there. She'll ask you to look, because you know what to look for: then kiss you: then ask you to buy her something there. She swears that she'll be happy with it, for years, but she needs it now, now the price is right. If you say you haven't the money in the house, she'll ask for a note of hand -and you're sorry you learnt to write. Why she asks doesn't she for money as if it's

维纳斯与马尔斯

把那些需要送礼物的日子视作禁忌日。你想逃避是徒劳的，她总会得到一些你的礼物，女人非常精通种种搜刮情人金钱的艺术。一个穿着长袍的商贩会到你情妇的家里去，她是准备购买的；他将坐在你的面前，摊开他的货品；于是她，为了给你一个显示你鉴赏力的机会，要求你为她看一看，随后她给你几个甜蜜的吻；随后她恳求你为她买几件。她会发誓说这些已够她用上几年了；而今天她正用得到；今天是一个机会。你说你身边没带钱是没用的，她会请你开一个票，那时你就会为你知书识字而懊悔了。当她为了要你的礼物，就像过生日似的预备好了点心时——而

her birthday, just for the cake, and how often it is her birthday, if she's in need? Why-she weeps doesn't she, mournfully, for a sham loss, that imaginary gem that fell from her pierced ear? They many times ask for gifts, they never give in return: you lose, and you'll get no thanks for your loss. And ten mouths with as many tongues wouldn't be enough for me to describe the wicked tricks of whores.

热恋中的男子

且这生日又是每次当她需要什么东西时要过的——怎么办呢？当她撒谎说她丢失了一件东西，面带忧愁的来到你面前，哭诉她丢失了一枚耳朵上的宝石时，怎么办呢？妇女们总向你要许多东西，而且她们会说不久就会还给你的；可是一旦到了她们的手中，你就再也不要奢望她们会还给你了。虽然你受了这样大的损失，但是别人却一点儿也不感激你。真的，即使是有十口十舌，我也不能数清那些娼妓的无耻伎俩。

Ⅻ: Write and Make Promises

Try wax to pave the way, pour it out on scraped tablets: let wax be your mind's true confidante. Bring her your flattering words and play the lover: and, whoever you are, add a humble prayer. Achilles was moved by prayer to grant Hector's body to Priam: a god's anger's deflected by the voice of prayer. Make promises: what harm can a promise do? Anyone can be rich in promises. Hope lasts, if she's once believed in, a useful, though deceptive, goddess. If you've given, you can quite reasonably be forgotten: she carried it off, and now she's nothing to lose. But if you don't give, always appear about to: like barren fields that always cheat the farmer, like the gambler who goes on losing, lest he's finally lost, and calls the dice back endlessly into his eager hand. This is the work, the labour, to have her without giving first: and she'll go on giving, lest she

12.书写承诺

先在几个精磨的板上写几句温柔的话语去探路。要让这第一封信札就使她知道你的心情。上面要写着殷勤的颂词和动情的话;而且不要管你是什么身份,你加上那最低微的恳求。海克笃尔的尸体之所以能够还给泊里阿摩思[90],也就是因为那老人的恳求打动了阿岂赖斯的心。神祇的愤怒都会被柔顺的声音所感动。答应吧,答应吧。这是值得的,任何人都是被允许的。当人们希望拥有信心时,能够长久一些:这是一个欺人的女神,但是却很有用。假如你送些礼物给你的情妇,你就会找不到便宜了:就是欺骗了你,她也不会有什么损失的。你总是要装着正要送她东西的样子,可是永远都不要送给她。不肥沃的田地就是这样经常欺骗它的主人;赌徒也就是这样在不再输的希望中不停地输,而偶然的运气又诱惑着他贪婪的手。那最难的一点,那精细的工作,就是不赠送礼物而得到

lose what she's freely given. So go on, and send your letter's flattering words, try her intention, test the road out first. Cydippe was deceived by the message the apple brought, and unaware the girl by her own words was caught.

I warn you, youths of Rome, learn the noble arts, not just to defend some trembling client: like the crowd, the grave judge, the elected senate, a woman will give her hand, won by eloquence. But let your powers be hidden, don't display your eloquence: let irksome words vanish from your speech. Who, but a mindless fool, declaims to his sweet friend?

海克笃尔

美人的眷顾：于是，她为了不虚掷她所赠予的东西的价值，她便不能拒绝了。将这满篇柔情的信札发出去，去试探她的心，去开一条路。几个写在苹果上的字欺骗了那绮第珮[91]，于是这不知内幕的少女在朗读它的时候，被她自己的言语所缚住了。

研究美文啊，青年罗马人，我这样给你们忠告；不仅是为了保护那战战兢兢的被告人。正如人民，严厉的审判官和从人民中选出来的元老院议员，女人也是会屈服于辩才的。可是你要将你诱惑的方法隐藏得很好，不要一下子就显露出你的饶舌来。一切乡村学究气的语句都不要用。除

A strong letter often causes her displeasure. Let your speech be credible, use ordinary words, flattering though, speak as if you were present. If she won't receive the letter, returns it un-read, stick to your plan, and hope she'll read it later. In time stubborn oxen come to the plough, in time the horse learns to suffer the bridle: constant use wears away an iron ring, the curved plough's lost to the endless furrow. What's harder than stone, softer than water? Yet soft water carves the hardest stone. Once steadfast

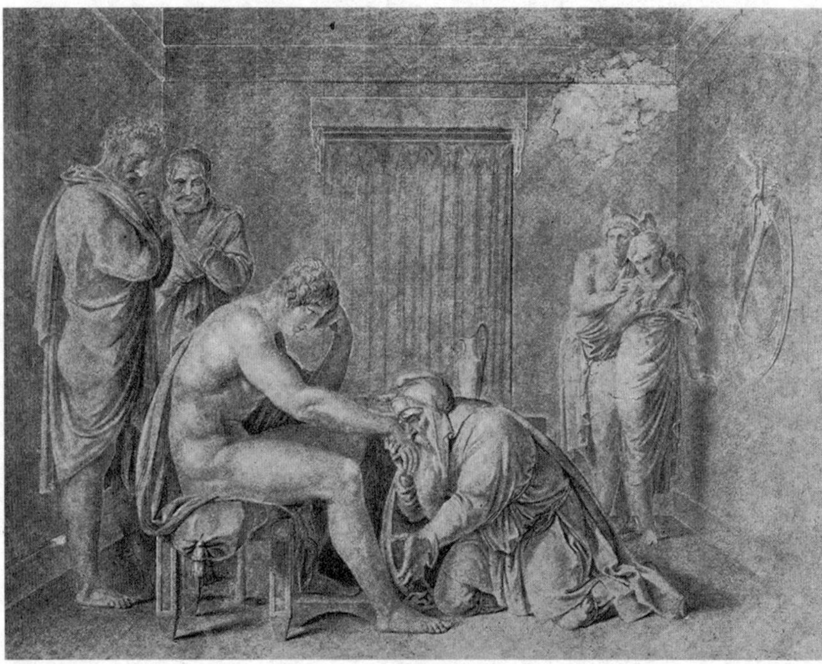

海克笃尔之父泊里阿摩思

了蠢人之外，谁会用一种演说者的口气写信给他的情妇呢？一封夸张的信是产生厌恶的主要原因。你的文体必须自然，你的词句必须简单，可是还要婉转，使别人在读你这封信的时候，好像听到了你的声音一样。假如她拒绝你的信札，连看也不看就送还你，你要相信她将会读它，你要坚持到底。不驯服的小牛终究是惯于驾犁的，倔犟的马日子久了终究会受制于辔头。在不停的摩擦之后，一个铁指环尚且会磨损。继续划着地，那弯曲的犁头终究会腐蚀磨损。还有什么能比石头更坚硬，比水更柔顺吗？可

you'll conquer Penelope herself in time: you'll see Troy captive, though it's captured late. She reads and won't reply? Don't press her: just let her keep on reading your flattery. If she wants to read, she'll want to answer what she's read: such things proceed by number and by measure. Perhaps at first a cool letter comes to you, asking: would you please not trouble her. What she asks, she fears: what she doesn't ask, she wants, that you go on; do it, and you'll soon get what you wish.

贞洁坚忍的珮耐洛珀

是柔水却能够滴穿坚石。即使是珮耐洛珀[92],只要你坚持到底,日子久了她也会屈服于你的,拜尔迦摩思[93]守了很长时间,可是终究还是被攻下了。譬如她读了你的信而不愿意回答你:那是她的自由。你只要使她继续读你的情书就可以了:她既然很愿意读,她不久就会愿意回答了。一切都是按部就班地来的。你或许会先接到一封不顺利的复信,在信上她请你停止追求。正当她求你不要惹她的时候,她却害怕你会照办,其实她是希望你能够坚持到底。追求啊,不久以后你就会如愿以偿了。

XⅢ: Be Where She Is

Meanwhile, if she's being carried, reclining on her bed, secretly approach your lady's litter, and to avoid offering your words to odious ears, hide what you can with skill and ambiguous gestures. If she's wandering at leisure in the spacious Colonnade, you join here there also, lingering, as a friend: now make as if to lead the way, now drop behind, now go on quickly, and now take it slow; don't be ashamed to slip amongst the columns, a while, then move along side by side; don't let her sit all beautiful in

荡秋千的情侣

13.如影随形

当你遇到你的情妇躺在她的舁床中时，你便走过去，好像是很偶然似的，而且害怕你的话语被一个不谨慎的人听了去，你便要尽你所能用模棱两可的手势来表达你的意思。假如她在一个广大的穹门下散步，你也应当走过去和她一起散步。有时走在她的前面，有时走在她的后面，有时加紧脚步，有时放慢脚步。你不要为了从人群中走出，从这个柱石赶到那个柱石下，紧贴着她走会让她害羞。不要让她独自一人仪态万方地坐在剧场中：在那

the theatre row without you: what you'll look at is the way she holds her arms. Gaze at her, to admire her is fine: and to speak with gestures and with glances. And applaud, the man who dances the girl's part: and favour anyone who plays a lover. When she rises, rise: while she's sitting, sit; pass the time at your lady's whim.

梳妆的裸女

里，她袒露的玉臂将给你一个动情的奇观；在那里，你可以凝视她，安闲地欣赏她，你可以向她打手势、抛媚眼。对那扮演少女的拟曲伶人喝彩[94]；对那扮演情人的演员则更要喝彩。她站起来时，你也要站起来；她如果一直坐着，你也坐着不要动：你必须懂得按照你情妇的兴致去消磨你的时间。

XⅣ: Look Presentable

Don't delight in curling your hair with tongs, don't smooth your skin with sharp pumice stone. Leave that to those who celebrate Cybele the Mother, howling wildly in the Phrygian manner. Male beauty's better for neglect: Theseus carried off Ariadne, without a single pin in his hair. Phaedra loved Hippolytus: he was unsophisticated; Adonis was dear to the goddess, and fit for the woods. Neatness pleases, a body tanned from

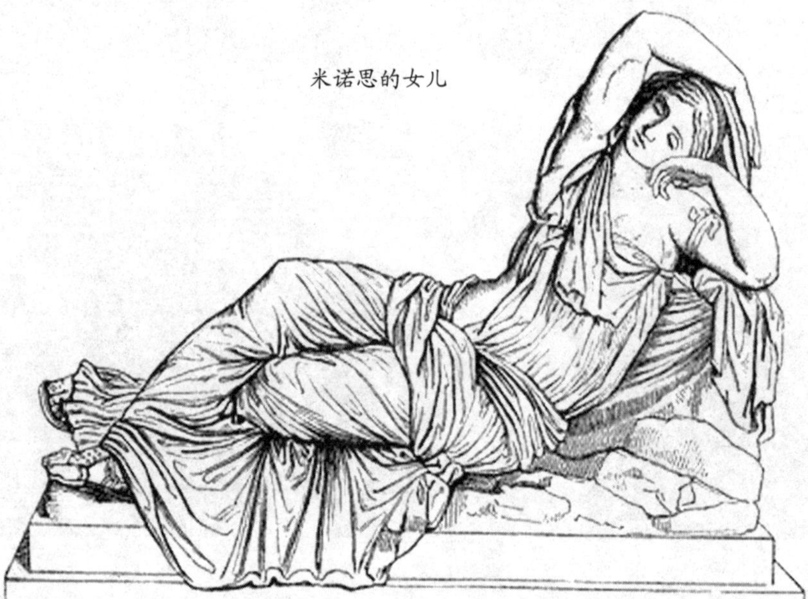
米诺思的女儿

14.外貌的学问

可是不要用热烙铁去烫你的头发,或者是用浮石去研你的皮肤。这些事,让那些用弗里基阿人的仪式唱着歌词歌颂启倍莱虞斯山女神的教士们[95]去做吧! 一种不加修饰的美对于男子来说是恰当的:当米诺思的女儿[96] 被戴设斯掠去的时候,戴设斯并没有将自己的头发用针簪在鬓边。伊包里度思虽然不注重外表的修饰,却仍然被弗特拉所爱[97]。那生活

exercise: a well fitting and spotless toga's good; no stiff shoe-thongs, your buckles free of rust, no sloppy feet for you, swimming in loose hide; don't mar your neat hair with an evil haircut; let an expert hand trim your head and beard. And no long nails, and make sure they're dirt-free; and no hairs please, sprouting from your nostrils. No bad breath exhaled from unwholesome mouth; don't offend the nose like a herdsman or his flock. Leave the rest for impudent women to do, or whoever's the sort of man who needs a man.

阿陶尼斯和维纳斯

在森林荒野中的阿陶尼斯终究还是得到了一个女神的心[98]。你必须爱清洁:不要害怕在马尔斯场锻炼身体而晒黑了你的皮肤;把你的宽袍弄得好好的,不要污迹。舌头上不要留一点儿舌苔,牙齿上也不要留一点儿齿垢。你的脚不要套着太大的鞋子;不要让你那修剪得不好的头发矗在你的头上,一定要请一位老练的理发师来整理你的头发和胡子;你的指甲必须剪得整齐而且干净;不要让鼻孔中的鼻毛露出来;不要让那难闻的气息从一张臭嘴里吐出来,当心不要让那公羊难闻的膻气使人作呕。其余的修饰,你就让那些年轻的媚娘或者那些反自然的男子和不要脸的男子去做吧!

XV：At Dinner Be Bold

Ah,Bacchus calls to his poet：he helps lovers too，and supports the fire with which he is inflamed. The frantic Cretan girl wandered the unknown sands，that the waters of tiny sea-borne Dia showed. Just as she was，from sleep，veiled by her loose robe，barefoot，with her brown hair unbound，she called，for cruel Theseus，to the unhearing waves，her gentle cheeks wet with tears of shame. She called，and wept as well，but both became her，she was made no less beautiful by her tears. Now striking her sweet breast with her hands，again and again，she cried:“That faithless man’s gone：what of me，now? What will happen to me?” she cried; and the whole shoreechoed to the sound of cymbals and frenzied drums. She fainted in terror，her next words were stifled：no sign of blood in her almost lifeless body. Behold! The Bacchantes with loose streaming

15.晚宴时的胆量

可是利倍尔开始招呼他的诗人了[99]，他也是保护有情人又加惠于那些正燃烧着爱情的人。格诺苏思的孩子[100]发狂地在荒滩上彷徨着，在第阿小岛[101]被海波冲击的地方。她刚从睡眠中脱身出来，只穿了一件薄薄的下衣，她的脚裸露着，她棕色的头发散披在她的肩头，她向那听不到她声音的海波哭诉戴设斯的残忍，而眼泪则满溢在那可怜的弃妇娇美的脸上。她又哭又喊，哭和喊对她来说都是很般配的：她的眼泪使她显得格外娇艳可人。那个不幸的人儿拍着胸脯说：“那负心人弃我而去了，我该怎么办呢？”她说：“我该怎么办呢？”忽然铙钹声在整个海岸上响起，狂热的手击打着鼓的声音也响起来了。她被吓倒了，而她的声音也停止了；她已经失去了知觉。那些披头散发的迷玛洛尼黛思们[102]来了；轻捷的刹帝鲁斯们[103]——神的先驱来了；酩酊大醉的老人西莱努思[104]来了：他被挂在因

hair: Behold! The wanton Satyrs, a crowd before the god: Behold! Old Silenus, barely astride his swaybacked mule, clutching tightly to its mane in front. While he pursues the Bacchae, the Bacchae flee and return, as the rascal urges the mount on with his staff. He slips from his long-eared mule and falls headfirst; the Satyrs cry: "Rise again, father, rise!" Now the God in his chariot, wreathed with vines, curbing his team of tigers, with golden reins; the girl's voice and colour and Theseus all lost; three times she tried to run, three times fear held her back. She shook, like a slender stalk of wheat stirred by the wind, and trembled like a light reed

跳神诸女

为重负而弯曲的驴子的鬣毛上，几乎就要跌下来了。当他追着那一边逃避他一边向他啰唆的跳神诸女时，当这个笨拙的骑士用木棒打着那只长耳兽的时候，他忽然滑了下来，跌了个倒栽葱。刹帝鲁斯高喊着："喂，起来啊，老伯伯，起来啊！"那时，神祇[105]正高坐在缠着葡萄蔓的车上，用金勒驾驭着那驯服的老虎。那少女把颜色、戴设斯的记忆和声音同时都失去了。她曾经三次想逃跑，可是恐惧的心理三次都缠住了她的脚。她战栗着，就像被风吹动的稻草和在沼泽中的芦苇一样。可是那神祇却对她说：

in a marshy pool. To whom the god said: "See, I come, more faithful in love; have no fear: Cretan, you'll be bride to Bacchus. Take the heavens for dowry; be seen as heavenly stars; and guide the anxious sailor often to your Cretan Crown." He spoke, and leapt from the chariot, lest she feared his tigers; the sand yielded under his feet; clasped in his arms (she had no power to struggle), he carried her away; all's easily possible to a god. Some sing "O Hymenaeus", some "Bacchus, euhoe!" So on the sacred bed the god and his bride meet. When Bacchus's gifts are set before you then, and you find a girl sharing your couch, pray to the father of feasts and nocturnal rites to command the wine to bring your head no harm. It's

沐浴的女神

"我是来向你贡献一个更忠诚的爱情的。不要怕,格诺苏思的女孩,你将会成为巴古斯的妻子。我将用天来作为你的礼物:在天上,你将成为一颗人们仰望的星,你灿烂的冠冕将成为没有把握的舵工的向导。"他这样说着,又怕那些老虎吓坏了阿丽亚特娜,便从车上跳下来(他的足迹印在地上),把那惊慌失措的公主紧抱在胸前,他将她举了起来。她怎么会抵抗呢?一个神祇的能力难道还有什么做不到的事情吗?跳神诸女们有的唱着催妆曲,有的喊着:"曷许思,曷荷艾。"[106]那年轻的新娘和神祇就这样

alright here to speak many secret things, with hidden words she'll feel were spoken for her alone: and write sweet nothings in the film of wine, so your girl can read them herself on the table; and gaze in her eyes with eyes confessing fire; you should often have silent words and speaking face. Be the first to snatch the cup that touched her lips, and where she drank from, that is where you drink; and whatever food her fingers touch, take that, and as you take it, touch hers with your hand. Let it be your wish besides to please the girl's husband: it'll be more useful to you to make friends. If you cast lots for drinking, give him the better draw: give him the garland you were crowned with. Though he's below you or beside you, let him always be served first: don't hesitate to second whatever he says. It's a safe well-trodden path to deceive in a friend's name, though it's a safe well-trodden path, it's a crime. That way the procurer procures far too much, and reckons to see to more than he was charged with. You'll be given sure limits for drinking by me: so pay attention to your mind and

在神圣的床榻上相合了。因此当你置身于有巴古斯礼物的华筵中时,假如一个女子坐在你的旁边,和你同坐在一张床榻上,你便祷告那在夜间供奉的夜的神祇[107],求他不要把你弄醉。于是你便可以用隐约的言语向她说出温柔的情话,她将毫不困难地猜度出你的意思来。用一点儿酒意画着多情的表情,使她可以在桌子上看出她是你心上的情妇,你的凝眸看着她的眼睛需要向她袒露出你的情焰。不需要语言,脸儿自有它雄辩的声音和语言。她的嘴唇啜过的酒杯你要第一个抢过来,而她喝过的那一边,你也要喝。她的手指所触过的一切菜肴,你都要去拿来,而在拿的时候,摸一摸她的手。你还需勉力去得到你美人的丈夫的欢心。在成为你的朋友之后,他对于你来说是很有用的。假如你抽到了筵席首座的签,你必须让给他;将那戴在你头上的王冠摘下来送给他;不管他的地位是卑于你或是和你平等,不要去管它,让他比你先上菜;而在谈话的时候,你还需要从容地将他的话重述一遍。最妥当、最普遍的欺骗方法,就是躲在友谊的名义后面,可是这方法虽然是十分妥当且十分普遍的,却总是一

feet. Most of all beware of starting a drunken squabble, and fists far too ready for a rough fight. Eurytion the Centaur died, made foolish by the wine; food and drink are fitter for sweet jests. If you've a voice, sing; if your limbs are supple, dance: and please, with whatever you do that's pleasing. And though drunkenness is harmful, it's useful to pretend; make your sly tongue stammer with lisping sounds, then, whatever you say or do that seems too forward, it will be thought excessive wine's to blame. And speak: "Well of your lady, speak well of the one she sleeps with." But silently in your thoughts wish the man ill.

Then when the table's cleared, the guests are free, the throng will

艾里谛洪

种罪过。在爱情上，一个受委任的人总比他的委任状要进一步，他自以为越权是他分内的事。喝酒的时候所应当遵守的原则是什么呢？我们就要指导你了。你的智慧和你的脚必须时常保持着平衡。尤其是要避免那些因酒而发生的争端，不要轻易和人家斗。不要学那愚蠢的因为饮酒过度而死亡的艾里谛洪[108]：筵席和酒只应当是温柔和欢快的。假如你的嗓子好，你就要歌唱；假如你的身段灵活，你就要跳舞；一切使人欢乐的，你都要一件件去做。真正的酒醉会让人感到讨厌，而一个假装的酒醉对于你来说却是十分有用的。你狡猾的舌头要"咯咯"地吐着不清楚的声音，这样一来，你所做的和你所说的即使有些大胆的地方，人们也都是可以原谅的。你应当说：

give you access to her and room. Join the crowd, and softly approach her, let fingers brush her thigh, and foot touch foot. Now's the time to speak to her: boorish modesty fly far from here; chance and V enus help the daring. Not from my rules your eloquence will come: desire her enough, you'll be fluent yourself. Your's to play the lover, imitate wounds with words: use whatever skill you have to win her belief. Don't think it's hard: each think's herself desired; the very worst take's pleasure in her looks. Yet often the imitator begins to love in truth, often, what was once imagined comes to be. Oh, be kinder to the ones who feign it, girls: true love will come, out of what was false. Now secretly surprise her mind with flatteries, as clear water undermines the hanging bank. Never weary of praising her face、her hair、her elegant fingers, and her slender feet. Even the chaste like their beauty to be commended: her form to even the virgin's pleasing and dear. Why is losing the contest in the Phrygian woodsa cause of shame to Juno and Pallas still? Juno's peacock shows his much-praised

"祝我所爱的人健康;祝和她同床的人健康。"可是在心里你却要诅咒她的丈夫立刻就死。

当酒阑客散的时候,那些客人就会给你接近你的美人的方法和机会。你夹在人群中,轻轻地靠近她,用你的手指捏着她的身体,用你的脚去碰她的脚。这便是交谈的时光:乡下气的羞态,走得远远的吧!机会和维纳斯只帮助胆大的人。像你那样会说话,当然就用不着来请教我们:只要想着开端,辩才便不需要思索,自然而然地来了。你应当扮演那个情郎的角色,而且在你的言语中,你需要做出受过爱情的伤的样子;要用尽种种方法使她坚信。要得到别人的信任并不是很难的事情,任何女人都自以为值得被爱。即使是那最丑的女子也会卖弄风姿。况且又有多少次起初只是装作在恋爱,而最终就真的恋爱了,从矫作到实现!年轻的美人们啊,请你们对那些做着爱情的外表给你们看的人们宽大些!这种爱情,起初是假装的,而以后却会变为诚恳的。你更可以用那些巧妙的阿谀偷偷地得到她的欢心,正如那水流不知不觉地淹没了那统治它的河岸一样。

plumage: if you watch in silence, he'll hide his wealth again. Race-horses between races on the testing course, love it when necks are patted, manes are combed.

智慧女神葩拉丝

你要毫不迟疑地去赞美她的姿容、她的头发、她那柔柔的手指和纤纤的脚。即使是最贞淑的女子听了对她赞美的谀词也是要动心的,容颜的美丽就是贞女也会注意的。裘娜和葩拉丝在弗里基阿树林中不就是因为这个缘故,直到如今还有意见吗[109]?你看那裘娜的鸟[110],假如你赞美它的翎羽,它便展开了;假如你默默地看着它,它便把它的宝物隐藏着。在赛车的时候,骏马是喜欢别人为它那梳得很好的鬣毛和优美的颈项喝彩的。

ⅩⅥ：Promise and Deceive

Don't be shy of promising: promises entice girls: add any gods you like as witness to what you swear. Jupiter on high laughs at lovers' perjuries, and orders Aeolus's winds to carry them into the void. Jupiter used to swear by the Styx, falsely, to Juno: now he looks favourably on his own example. Gods are useful: as they're useful, let's think they're there: take wine and incense to the ancient altars; indifferent calm and it's like, apathy, don't chain them: live innocently; the divine is close at hand; pay what you owe, hold dutifully to agreements; commit no fraud; let your hands be free from blood. Delude only women, if you're wise, with impunity; where truth's more to be guarded against than fraud. Deceive deceivers; for the most part an impious tribe; let them fall themselves into the traps they've set. They say in Egypt the life-giving waters failed in the

16.诺言与欺骗

你需要大胆地发誓，因为打动女人的是誓言，让一切神祇来为你的诚恳作证。裘比德在天上看着那些发着假誓的情人们发笑，又将这些假誓像玩具一样让艾沃鲁司[11]的臣仆带去撤销了。裘比德也经常对着司底克思[12]向裘娜立假誓：他在今天当然要加惠于那些学他的人们。诸神祇的存在是有用的。而且，因为有用，我们也就暂且相信他们是存在的吧。在他们祭坛的前面我们应该浪费我们的香和酒。他们不是沉浸在一个没有知觉的、和睡眠相似的休憩中。你要过一种纯洁的生活，神祇一直在看着你。偿还那些你欠别人的东西，忠实地遵守约定，千万不要作恶，你的手要清洁，不要染着人类的血。假如你是聪明人，你只能欺骗女人。你这样做可以是无罪的，只要你是出于诚意的。欺骗那些曾经欺骗过你的人

fields; and there were nine years of drought, then Thrasius came to Busiris, and said that Jove might be propitiated by shedding a stranger's blood. Busiris told him: "You become Jove's first victim, and you be the stranger to give Egypt water." And Phalaris roasted impetuous Perillus's body in the brazen bull: the unhappy creator was first to fill his work. Both cases were just: for there's no fairer law than that the murderous maker should perish by his art. As liars by liars are rightfully deceived, wounded by their own example, let women grieve.

司底克思

们。大部分的女子都是不诚实的，她们设下了陷阱，让她们自己坠下去吧！有人说埃及曾经一连九年大旱，一滴雨水都没有。于是德拉西乌思[113]找到蒲西里思[114]，对他说只有他才能够平息裘比德的怒气，只要在裘比德的祭坛上浇上一个异乡人的血就好了。蒲西里思回答他说："很好，你将会成为供献给裘比德的第一个牺牲品，你将会成为把雨水带给埃及的异乡人。"法拉里思[115]让人在铜牛中烧死残忍的培里鲁思[116]，那个不幸的发明者用自己的血浇灌着他亲手作出的成绩。这就是公正具有两面性的例子！其实将罪恶的制造者用他们自己所造的东西来处死是再公正不过的了。以虚假的誓言来回答虚伪的誓言是公平的法则。那欺诈的女人也应当受到同样的欺诈！

ⅩⅦ: Tears, Kisses, and Take the Lead

And tears help: tears will move a stone; let her see your damp cheeks if you can. If tears (they don't always come at the right time) fail you, touch your eyes with a wet hand. What wise man doesn't mingle tears with kisses? Though she might not give, take what isn't given. Perhaps she'll struggle, and then say "you're wicked": struggling she still wants, herself, to be conquered. Only, take care her lips aren't bruised by snatching, and that she can't complain that you were harsh. Who takes a kiss, and doesn't take the rest, deserves to lose all that were granted too. How much short of your wish are you after that kiss? Ah me, that was boorishness stopped you not modesty. Though you call it force: it's force that pleases girls; what delights is often to have given what they wanted, against their will. She who is taken in love's sudden onslaughtis pleased,

17.用眼泪、亲吻来驾驭感情

眼泪也是有用的:它能够软化金刚石。你需要让你的情人看见你泪流满面。可是当你流不出眼泪的时候(因为眼泪不是随叫随到的),你就要用你的手将你的眼眶儿弄湿了。哪一个有经验的男子不会把接吻混到情语中去呢?你的美人儿如果拒绝,就让她拒绝吧,你做你的就是了。起初她或许还会抵抗,会叫你"坏坯子";可是当她在抗拒的时候,她其实在心里已经愿意屈服了。可是你不要用笨拙的接吻碰痛了她娇嫩的唇儿,给她一个说你粗蛮的借口。你得到一个亲吻而不去得到其余的,你就错失了她给予你的恩惠。在接吻之后,你还等着什么来实现你的一切心愿呢?多么可怜啊!牵制住你的不是羞耻,却是一种愚昧的笨拙。你会说,这不是对她施行强暴了吗?可是这种强暴正是妇人所喜欢的。她们喜欢

and finds wickedness is a tribute. And she who might have been forced, and escapes unscathed, will be saddened, though her face pretends delight. Phoebe was taken by force: force was offered her sister; and both, when raped, were pleased with those who raped them. Though the tale's known, it's still worth repeating, how the girl of Scyros mated Achilles the hero. Now the lovely goddess had given her fatal bribe to defeat the other two beneath Ida's slopes: now a daughter-in-law had come to Priam from an enemy land; a Greek wife in Trojan walls. All swore the prescribed oath to the injured husband: now one man's grief became a nation's cause.

思凯洛斯的少女

给人的东西,她们也愿意人们去夺取。爱情的盗窃和强力取得的妇人反而享受这种盗窃，这种蛮横在她们看来就像是送给她们的礼物一样称心。当她从别人袭击她的挣扎中无瑕地脱身时,她可以在脸上装作很快活,其实却是满肚子的不高兴。菲珮[117]曾经受过强暴,她的妹妹也做过强暴的牺牲品,可是她们两个却并非不爱那对她们实施强暴的人。一个大家都知道的故事,可是却很值得讲一讲,那就是思凯洛斯的少女[118]和海木尼阿的英雄[119]结合。在伊达山上,那个女神[120]已经对她的敌人高唱凯歌了,并且报答了称赞她最美的人[121],一个新媳妇儿已经从遥远的地方

Shamefully, though he gave way to a mother's prayer, Achilles hid his manhood in women's clothes. What's this, Aeacides? Spinning's not your work: your search for fame's through Pallas's other arts. Why the basket? Your arm's meant to bear a shield: why does the hand that will slay Hector hold the yarn? Throw away the spindle wound laboriously with thread! The spear from Pelion's to be brandished by this hand. By chance a royal virgin shared the room: through her rape she learned he was a man. That she was truly won by force, we must think; but she still wanted to be won by force. She often cried: "Stop!" afterwards, when Achilles hurried on: now he'd taken up stronger weapons than the distaff.

美奈拉乌思

来到泊里阿摩斯的家中了，而在伊里雍[122]的城垣中已经关进了一个希腊的妻子。全希腊的王侯都发誓要为受侮辱的丈夫[123]报仇：因为对一个人的侮辱已经变成了对大家的侮辱。那时阿岂赖斯（假如他听到母亲的请求，那是多么的羞耻啊）把自己的男性特征隐藏在妇人穿着的长衫里[124]。你做什么啊，艾阿古斯的孙子[125]？纺羊毛不是你的本分。你应当从葩拉丝[126]的另一种艺术中找到你的光荣。这些做女红的篮子你管它干吗？你的手是注定要拿盾的。为什么你手拿着梭子？难道要用这个扑倒海克笃尔吗？把这个纺锤丢得远一些，你的手是应该举起贝利翁山的矛[127]的。有朝一日，在同一张床上睡着

Where's that force now? Why do you restrain the perpetrator of your rape, Deidamia? No doubt as there's a sort of shame in having started first, so it's pleasant to have what someone else has started. Ah! The youth has too much faith in his own beauty, if he waits until she asks him first. The man must approach first: speak the words of entreaty; she courteously receives his flattering prayers. To win her, ask her: she only wants to be asked; give her the cause and the beginning of your longing. Jupiter went as a suppliant to the heroines of old: no woman ever seduced great Jupiter. If you find she disdains the advent of your prayerful sighs, leave off what you've begun, retrace

阿岂赖斯

一个王侯的女儿[128];她发现她的伴侣是一个男子,于是她被强暴了。她是屈服于武力的(至少应当这样想),可是她并不是因为屈服于武力而发怒。当阿岂赖斯要匆匆离去的时候,她对他说:“不要走。”因为那时阿岂赖斯已经放下梭子去取兵器了。那个所谓的“强暴”哪里去了?黛伊达米亚,你为什么用一种爱抚的语气来挽留带给你羞辱的人呢?是的,羞耻心禁止女人主动爱抚男子,但是当男子先去爱抚她的时候,她是非常喜欢的。当然,少年对于自己的体格美有一种太过于自负的信心,他等着女子先上手。应当是男子开始的,应当是男子来说那些祷词的。他爱情的祈祷便会被她很好地接受了。你要得到她吗?祈求吧!

your steps. What shuns them, they desire the more: they hate what's there; remove her loathing by pursuing less. The hoped-for love should not always be declared: introduce desire hidden in the name of friendship. I've seen the most severe of women fooled this way: he who once was a worshipper, became a lover.

爱神之吻

她只希望这种请求。向她解释你爱情的原因和来历。裘比德恳求着走向传说中的女英雄们，不管他如何伟大，没有一个女子会先来挑拨他的。可是如果你的恳求撞在一种轻蔑别人的骄傲的厌恶上，你就不要再坚持了，转过身来。多少女子喜欢那些奉承她们的人而厌恶那些专心侍奉她们的人！不要太性急，那样你就不会被人厌恶了。在你的请求中不要常常泄露出达到最后目的的希望；如果想让你的爱情渗透到她的心里，你就必须戴着友谊的假面具。我看见过许多桀骜不驯的美人都受了这种驭制法的骗：她们的朋友不久就变成了她们的情人。

XⅧ: Be Pale: Be Wary of Your Friends

A pale colour would shame a sailor on the ocean wave, who's blackened by the rays of the sun: and shame the farmer who turns the soil with curved plough and heavy harrow, underneath the heavens. And you who seek the athlete's crown, you too would be ashamed if all your body was white. Let all lovers be pale: it's the colour fitting for love; it suits, though fools have thought it of no value. Orion wandered pale, for Side, in the woods, Daphnis was pale for his reluctant Naiad. Let your lean-

美丽的猎人奥里雍

18.警惕你的朋友

一张雪白的脸儿和水手是不般配的:海水和日光准会过早地把他的脸儿弄成褐色。它和农夫也是不般配的,因为农夫总是在露天之下,用犁头或是重耙开垦泥土。而你也是一样的,你是在游艺中谋得橄榄冠的人,生着雪白的皮肤是你的羞耻。可是一切多情的人都应该是惨白的。因为惨白是爱情的病症,那才是和他相称的颜色。许多人都认为这并不是没用的。奥里雍[129]是惨白的,当他被西黛[130]所爱,在树林中彷徨的时候,惨白的达夫尼思[131]被一个无情的水仙所爱。你更要用你的消瘦显露出你内心

ness show your heart: don't think it a shame to slip a cape over your shining hair; let youthful limbs be worn away by sleepless nights and care, and the grief of a great love. To gain your desire, be miserable, and those who see you can say: "You're in love."

Should I lament, warn you perhaps that right and wrong are confused by all? Friendship and loyalty empty words. Ah me, it's not safe to praise your love to a friend: if he believes your praise, he'll steal her himself. But Patroclus never disgraced Achilles's bed: and how modest Phaedra was with Pirithous. Pylades l oved Hermione,

田园诗人达夫尼思

的苦痛，还要不怕羞地用病人用的包头布将你光耀的头发裹住。那由一种剧烈的爱生发出来的不眠、烦虑、苦痛使一个青年人消瘦。为了达成你的心愿，你要使别人可怜你，要使人一看见你就会脱口而出："你是在恋爱吧！"

如今我是应该缄默呢，还是应该含愁地看着德行和罪恶相混呢？友谊、善意，都只是空虚的字眼儿。啊！你向你的友人夸耀你所爱着的人是非常危险的事，假如他相信了你的颂词，他立刻就会变成你的对手了。有人要对我说："可是那阿克笃尔的孙子并没有玷污阿岂赖斯的床呀；

just as Phoebus Pallas, or as Castor was twin to you Pollux. Who hopes for that, hopes for apple-bearing tamarisks, and looks for honey in the middle of the stream. All delight in what's shameful: care only for their pleasures, and are pleased too when trouble comes to others. Ah it's a crime! It's not their rivals that lovers fear: flee those you think are friends, and you'll be safe. Beware of brothers, relatives, and dear friends: that crowd offers you true cause for fear.

比里都思

弗特拉虽然不忠实,比里都思[132]却没有什么举动呀;比拉代思[133]爱着海尔迷奥奈[134],他的爱情就像斐菩斯对葩拉丝,或者迦思笃尔和保鲁克思对登达勒思的女儿[135]的爱情一样纯洁。”在今天相信这种奇谈,不亚于希望西河柳结果子或者是到江心去找蜜。罪犯有多少香饵啊!每个人都是为了谋取自身的欢乐,品尝别人的欢乐是格外有味道的。这是多么可耻的啊!一个有情人所要顾忌的倒不是他的仇敌。你要高枕无忧,你就应该避开那些你以为对你很忠实的朋友。亲戚、弟兄、至友,全都是不可信任的:这些都是会给你带来极大恐惧的人。

ⅩⅨ: Be Flexible

I've done, but there's diversity in women's hearts: a thousand minds require a thousand methods. One soil doesn't bear all crops: vines here are good; olives there; this teems with healthy wheat. There are as many manners of heart as kinds of face: a wise man will adapt to many forms, and like Proteus now, melt into the smooth waters, now be a tree, now a

众神欢聚

19.灵活掌握

我就要结束了,可是我要说,女子的脾气都不是完全一样的。对于这种种不同的性格,你要用千种方法去引诱。同一块土地也不能生出所有的产品:有的适宜种植葡萄,有的适宜种植橄榄,有的则是种植小麦才会有好的收成。人心不同就如同人的面貌不同。伶俐的男子能够屈就各种的不同,就像有时可以变作轻波,有时变作狮子,有时变作像长着坚毛的野猪迫洛德思[136]一样的脾气。有的鱼是用鱼叉叉到的,有的鱼是用钩子

lion, now a bristling boar. These fish are speared, those caught on a hook: others trawled in billowing nets with straining ropes. One mode won't suit you for every age-group: the older hinds spot a trap from further off. If the simple find you cunning, and the modest crude, the poor things will straightaway mistrust themselves. So it happens that she who fears to trust an honest man, falls to the embrace of some low rascal.

Part of my task is left: part of the labour's done. Moor my boat here to the anchor-chains.

海神迫洛德思

钓的,有的鱼是用网捕捞的。总是用一个方法是不会成功的,应当按照你情妇的年龄去变通。一头老牝鹿能够在很远的地方就发现别人为它设下的陷阱。假如你在一个初出茅庐的女子面前显得太狡猾,或者是在一个忸怩的女子面前显得太冒险,她就会立刻不信任你,而小心防范着你了。所以那些害怕委身于一个规矩男子的女子总是坠入一个浪子的怀抱中。

我的一部分工程已经做完,只剩下另外一部分要做了。现在我们暂且抛下锚停住我们的船吧!

第二卷　如何保持爱情

Book Ⅱ　How to maintain love

I: His Task

Sing out the Paean: sing out the Paean twice! The prize I searched for falls into my net. Delighted lovers grant my songs the palm, I'm preferred to Hesiod and old Homer. So Paris the stranger sailed, from hostile Amyclae's shore, under white sheets, with his ravished bride: such was Pelops who brought you home Hippodamia, borne on the foreign wheels of his conquering car. What's your hurry, young man? Your boat's mid ocean, and the harbour I search for is far away. It's not enough the girl's come to you, through me, the poet: she's captured by my art, she's to be kept by my art too. There's no less virtue in keeping than in finding. There's chance in the latter: the first's a work of art.

Now aid me, your follower, Venus, and the Boy, and Erato, Muse, now you have love's name too. Great my task as I try to tell what arts can

1.他的任务

唱"伊奥·拜盎！"[137]呀，再唱一遍"伊奥·拜盎！"呀！我所追求的猎物已经投入我的罗网中了。欢乐的情人，把一个绿色的月桂冠戴在了我的头上，又将我举到阿斯克拉的老人[138]和梅奥尼阿的盲人[139]之上。正如那失掉了尚武精神的阿米克莱城[140]，顺利地将东道主的妻子[141]带走了的泊里阿摩思的儿子[142]一样；就像希苞达米亚[143]，把你载在胜利的车上，将你带到异国去的人[144]一样。青年人你为什么如此性急啊？你的船还在大海的中央，离我要带你去的港口还很远啊！我的诗还不能达到把你所爱的人儿放在你怀里的目的：我的艺术使你取得她，我的艺术也应当使你长久拥有她。得到胜利和保持胜利是同样需要才能的。还有一点要靠机会，另外一点则完全靠我的艺术了。

现在，岂带拉的女神[145]和你的儿子[146]，请你们帮助我吧！现在，你，爱

make Love stay: that boy who wanders so, through the vast world. And he's flighty, and has two wings on which he vanishes: it's a tricky job to pin him down. Minos blocked every road of flight for his guest: but Daedalus devised a bold winged path. When he'd imprisoned the offspring of its mother's sin, the man half-bull, the bull who was half-man, he said: "Minos, the Just, let my exile end; let my native land receive my ashes. And since I couldn't live in my own country, driven from it by cruel fate, still let me die there. Give my boy freedom, if the father's service was

盲诗人荷马

拉陀[147],也请你帮助我啊,因为你的名字是从爱情来的!我正计划着一个大的事业,我将告诉人们用哪一种艺术,可以固定阿谟尔,那个不停地在宇宙中飞翔着的浮躁的孩子。他是轻盈的,他有一双能使他脱逃的翅膀;不让他飞翔是很困难的事情。米诺思为了防止他的宾客逃走[148],在所有的路上都设下防备,可是这客人却用翅膀开辟了一条新路。当代达鲁思把那个犯罪母亲的爱情果子,半人半牛的怪物关起来以后,便对米诺思说:"米诺思啊,你是凡人中最公正的,请你让我回去吧!让我的骨灰葬在我的故土中吧!做了不公正命运的牺牲者,我不能生活在我的乡土中,至少请你准许我死在那里。假如那老

worthless; or if power will not spare the child, let it spare the old." He spoke the words, but they, and so many others, were in vain: his freedom was still de-nied him by the king. When he realised this, he said: "Now, now, O Dae-dalus, you have an object for your skilfulness. Minos rules the earth and the waves: neither land or sea is open for my flight. The sky road still remains: we'll try the heavens. Jupiter, on high, favour my plan: I don't aspire to touch the starry spheres; there is no way to flee the king but this. I'd swim the Stygian waves, if Styx offered me a path: through my nature new laws are mine." Trouble often sharpens the wits: who would think any man could travel by the air-roads? He lays out oar-like wings

希芭达米亚

人不能够得到你的恩准，那么就请准许我的儿子回去吧；假如你不肯赦免这个孩子，那么就请你赦免老人吧！"他这样说，可是尽管他说了千遍万遍，米诺思始终不允许他回去。知道恳求是无济于事的，他心里想："代达鲁思，一个显示你身手的机会来了。米诺思是陆上的主人、水上的主人。陆和水是我们都无法脱逃的。只剩下空间这一条路了，我应当从哪里开辟我的路呢？统治诸天的裘比德啊，请赦免我的企图。我并不奢望升到你的天宫上去，可是要逃离我的暴君，除了你的领域没有第二条路啊！假如司底克思[149]可以给我们一条路，我们早就穿过司底克思的水了。然而既然是无路可走，我便不得不变换我的

with lines of feathers, and ties the fragile work with fastenings of string, and glues the ends with beeswax melted in the flames, and now the work of this new art's complete.Laughing, his son handled the wax and feathers not knwing they were being readied for his own shoulders. His father said of them: "This is the art that will take us home, by this creation we'll escape from Minos. Minos bars all other ways but can not close the skies: as is fitting, my invention cleaves the air. But don't gaze at the Bear, that

文艺女神爱拉陀

本能了。"才能常常是被不幸所唤醒的。谁会相信人可以在空中旅行呢？可是代达鲁思却用翎羽制造了翼翅,用麻线绑缚住;又用熔蜡胶固了底部。于是那个新的机械就制作完毕了。那个孩子欢乐地用手转着羽毛和蜡,不知道这个家伙是为他准备的。他的父亲对他说:"这就是送我们回去的唯一的船,这是我们逃离米诺思的唯一方法。他即使是断了我们的一切归路,他总不能断了我们空间的路。我们还有空间啊。用我的发明冲破那空间！可是你不能看代格阿的处女[150]和鲍沃代思[151]的伴侣,还有

Arcadian girl, or Bootes's companion, Orion with his sword: fly behind me with the wings I give you; I'll go in front; your job's to follow; you'll be safe where I lead. For if we go near the sun through the airy aether, the wax will not endure the heat; if our humble wings glide close to ocean, the breaking salt waves will drench our feathers. Fly between the two: and fear the breeze as well, spread your wings and follow, as the winds allow." As he warns, he fits the wings to his child, shows how they move, as a bird teaches her young nestlings. Then he fastened the wings he'd fashioned to his own shoulders, and poised his anxious body for the strange path. Now, about to fly, he gave the small boy a kiss, and the

鲍沃代思

拿着剑的奥里雍。跟着我飞，我将飞在你前面，由我带领着，你就可以平安无事了。假如在飞行的时候我们升得太高，靠近了太阳，蜡是不耐热的；假如降得太低，靠近了大海，我们的翅膀又会被打湿而不能活动了。要飞在两者之间，而且还应当留心风。我的儿子，你必须顺着它的方向飞去。"他一边教导，一边把翅膀绑在他儿子的身上，又教他如何拍动，就像老鸟在教小鸟一样，随后把自己的翅膀绑在肩上，小心翼翼地飘荡在他所开辟的新路上。在要飞行之前，他把他的儿子吻了许多次，而那眼泪还是忍不住，在他的脸颊上肆意

tears ran down the father's cheeks. A small hill, no mountain, higher than the level plain: there their two bodies were given to the luckless flight. And Daedalus moved his wings, and watched his son's, and all the time kept to his own course. Now Icarus delights in the strange journey, and, fear forgotten, he flies more swiftly, with daring art. A man catching fish, with quivering rod, saw them, and the task he'd started dropped from his hand. Now Samos was to the left (Naxos was far behind and Paros, and

代格阿的处女

地流淌。在那不远的地方有一座山冈，虽然比山低，却要高出平原。他们便在那里开始他们冒险的逃亡。代达鲁思一边拍着翅膀，一边回头看他儿子的翅膀，可是却一点儿也没有耽搁他的空间旅行。他们路上见到的新奇已经蛊惑住他们了。不久伊迦鲁思就什么恐慌也没有了，他越飞越起劲。一个用细弱的芦竿钓鱼的渔夫看见了他们，把钓到的鱼儿都丢下了。他们已经在左边过了刹摩斯[152]（拿克若斯[153]、巴罗斯[154]和为克拉里乌

Delos beloved by Phoebus the god) Lebinthos lay to the right, and shady-wooded Calymne, and Astypalaea ringed by rich fishing grounds, when the boy, too rash, with youth's carelessness, soared higher, and left his father far behind. The knots give way, and the wax melts near the sun, his flailing arms can't clutch at thin air. Fearful, from heaven's heights he gazes at the deep: terrified, darkness, born of fear, clouds his eyes. The wax dissolves: he thrashes with naked arms, and flutters there with nothing to support him. He falls, and falling cries:"Father, oh father, I'm lost!" the salt-green sea closes over his open lips. But now the unhappy father, his father, calls,"Icarus! Where are you Icarus, where under the sky?" Calling "Icarus",he saw the feathers on the waves. Earth holds his bones: the waters take his name.

思所爱的代罗斯[155]都落在他们后面了),在他们的右边已经飞过了莱班托斯[156]、布满森林的加林奈[157]和被很多渔场环绕的阿思底巴拉艾[158],忽然那个胆大的青年人向很高的天上飞去,离开了他的父亲。他翅膀的连接处松了,蜡在飞近太阳的时候熔化了,他徒劳地摇动着他的手臂,他无法在稀薄的空中把持住自己的身体。他在空中充满恐惧地望着大海,那使他战栗的恐怖用黑暗把他的眼睛蒙住了。蜡已经完全熔化了。他拍动着空空的两臂,他震颤着却又无可依托,便坠了下来。在他坠下去的时候,他高喊着:"我的爸爸啊,我的爸爸啊,我被拖下去了!"当他说这话的时候,绿波把他的嘴掩住了。这时他可怜的父亲(啊,他从此不再是人父了)喊着:"伊迦鲁思!伊迦鲁思!你在哪儿,你飞到哪里去了?"当他看见羽毛漂浮在海水上时,他还喊着"伊迦鲁思"。大地已经接受了伊迦鲁思的遗骸,大海保留着他的名字。

Ⅱ: You Need Gifts of Mind

Minos could not hold back those mortal wings: I'm setting out to check the winged god himself. He who has recourse to Thracian magic, fails, to what the foal yields, torn from its new-born brow, Medea's herbs can't keep love alive, nor Marsian dirges mingled with magic chants. If incantations only could enslave love, Ulysses would have been tied to Circe, Jason to the Colchian. It's no use giving girls pale drugs: drugs hurt the mind, have power to cause madness.

Away with such evils: to be loved be lovable: something face and form alone won't give you. Though you're Nireus loved by Homer of old, or sweet Hylas ravished by the Naiades' crime, to keep your love, and not to find her leave you, add gifts of mind to grace of body. A sweet form is fragile, what's added to its yearslessen it, and time itself eats it away.

2.丰富你的智慧

米诺思不能禁止一个凡人凭借翼翅逃走,而我却要缚住一个飞翔的神祇[159]!想借海木尼阿的法术[160]或者是用那从小马头上割下来的东西[161]的人实在是错误的。为了使爱情经久不衰,美黛阿[162]的草是没有用的,马尔西人[163]的毒药和魔术也全都没有用了。假如魔法能够维持爱情,那么生在法西斯河畔的公主[164]早就可以留住艾松的儿子[165]了,启尔凯[166]也早就可以留住屋里赛思了。所以给少女喝春药是没有用的:春药扰乱了她们的理性而使她们疯狂。

不要用这些有罪的方法吧!你应当是可爱的,别人自然也就会爱你了。如果只有面貌或身材的美是远远不够的,即使你是老荷马所赞赏的尼勒思[167],或者是那邪恶的拿牙黛丝们偷去的希拉思[168]。假如你要保留你的情妇而不希望被抛弃的话,你就应当发挥身体的长处,还要加上智

Violets and open lilies do not flower forever, and thorns are left stiffening on the blown rose. And white hair will come to find you, lovely lad, soon wrinkles will come, furrowing your skin. Then nourish mind, which lasts, and adds to beauty: it alone will stay till the funeral pyre. Cultivate your thoughts with the noble arts, more than a little, and learn two languages. Ulysses wasn't handsome, but he was eloquent, and still racked the seagoddesses with love. How often Calypso mourned his haste, and denied the waves were fit for oars! She asked him again and again about the fall of Troy: He grew

魔女美黛阿

慧。美是一个容易消残的东西：它随着岁月一年一年地消减下去；它一年一年不停地毁坏下去，紫罗兰和百合不是永远都开着花的；而蔷薇一旦凋谢，它的空枝上就只剩下刺了。你也是这样的，美丽的青年人，你的头发不久也会变白的；你的脸颊不久也会爬上皱纹。现在就要培养你的智慧，它才是最经久的，而且可以成为你美的依赖：它是可以陪伴你到坟墓的唯一瑰宝。勤勉地去研究美术和两种语言[169]。屋里赛思并不英俊，但是他是一个善长辞令的人；这个就已经足够使两位海上女神[170]因为他而朝思暮想了。

used to retelling it often, differently. They walked the beach: there, lovely Calypso too emanded the gory tale of King Rhesus's fate. He, with a rod (a rod perhaps he already had) illustrated what she asked in the thick sand. "This," he said, "is Troy" (drawing the walls in the sand); "This your Simois: imagine this is our camp. This is the field," (he drew the field), "that was dyed with Dolon's blood, while he spied on Achilles's horses. here were the tents of Thracian Rhesus: Here am I riding back the captured horses at night." And he was drawing more, when suddenly a

美少年希拉思

珈丽泊苏[171]多少次因为看见他匆忙要动身而悲啼，坚决地对他说海浪不容许他开船！她不停地要求他讲特洛伊没落的故事，那故事我换了不同的说法不知讲过多少次了。有一天，他们在海滩上停止了脚步：在那里，那美丽的珈丽泊苏要听奥特里赛人首领[172]流血的结果。他便用那支他偶然拿在手中的轻轻的小杖为她在沙上绘画。他一边画着城墙一边说："这就是特洛伊城。这是西莫伊斯[173]：譬如说我的营地在那儿。过去就是一片平原（他又画了一片平原），那就是我们杀死道隆[174]的地方，他试图在夜里盗窃海木尼阿英雄[175]的马，那边搭着西笃尼于思人雷梭思[176]的营帐，我在

wavewashed away Troy, and Rhesus, and his camp. Then the goddess said "Do you see what you place your trust in for your voyage, waves that have destroyed such mighty names?" So listen, whoever you are, fear to rely on treacherous beauty or own to something more than just the flesh.

水神珈丽珀苏

夜里从那儿盗了他的马。"他正要画其他的东西,忽然打过来一片波浪,把特洛伊、雷梭思的营帐和雷梭思本人都带走了。于是那位女神便对他说:"你还敢相信这在你眼前抹去如此伟名的海水能够送你回去吗?"因此,随便你怎样,总不要相信托那斯人的美貌,要在身体的长处上增加其他的长处。

Ⅲ: Be Gentle and Good Tempered

Gentleness especially impresses minds favourably: harshness creates hatred and fierce wars. We hate the hawk that lives its life in battle, and the wolf whose custom is to raid the timid flocks. But the swallow, for its gentleness, is free from human snares, and Chaonian doves have dovecotes to live in. Away with disputes and the battle of bitter tongues: sweet love must feed on gentle words. Let married men and married women be checked by rebuffs, and think in turn things always are against them: that's proper for wives; quarrelling's the marriage dowry; but a mistress should always hear the longed-for cooing. No law orders you to come together in one bed: in your rules it's love provides the entertainment. Approach her with gentle flatteries and words to delight her ear, so that your arrival makes her glad. I don't come as a teacher of love for the rich:

3.温柔与好脾气

最得人心的是那熟练的殷勤。狡猾和尖刻的话只能让人产生憎恨。我们厌恶那以斗为生的鹰隼和那专扑弱羊的狼，可是我们绝对不会张网捕捉那些无害的燕子。而在塔上，我们让那卡屋尼阿的鸟儿[17]自由地居住着。把那些口角和伤人的话放得远一些：温柔的话是爱情的养料。妻子离开丈夫，丈夫离开妻子都是因为口角：他们以为这样做是理所应当的，妻子的妆奁，那就是口角，至于情妇呢，她应该能够常常听见中听的话。你们同睡在一张床上并不是法律规定的；属于你的法律，就是爱情。你要带着温存的抚爱和多情的言语去亲近你的昵友，使她一看见你就觉得快活。我不是为有钱人教授爱术的；愿意出钱的人是用不着我的教导的。他们是不需要什么智慧的，当他要的时候，他只要说“收下这个吧”就足够了。对于这种人我是只好让步的：他们获取别人欢心的方法比我强得多。我的这部诗作

he who can give has no need of my art; He has genius who can say:"Take this." when he pleases: I submit: he delights more than my inventions. I'm the poor man's poet, who was poor when I loved: when I could give no gifts, I gave them words. The poor must love warily: the poor fear to speak amiss, and suffer much that the rich would not. I remember mussing my lady's hair in anger: how many days that anger cost me! I don't think I tore her dress, I didn't feel it: but she said so, and my reward was to replace it. But you, if you're wise, avoid your teacher's faults, and fear the harm that came from my offence. Make war with the Parthians, peace with a civilised friend, and laughter, and whatever engenders love.

巴尔底人

是专为穷人们创作的,因为我自己也有穷困的时候,我曾经恋爱过。当我不能送礼物的时候,我便把美丽的语言送给我的情妇。穷人在爱情中应当具有深心;他应当避免说一些不适当的话;他应当忍受一个有钱的情人所不能忍受的许多事情。我记得有一次在发怒的时候,我把我情妇的头发弄乱了;那次发怒损失了我多少幸福的日子啊!我不相信我撕碎了她的衫子,而且我也没有看见,可是她却坚决那样说,于是我不得不花钱赔了她一件。可是你们,假如你们是聪明的,就避免你们教师的过失吧,而且也像我一样地担心遭受苦痛的煎熬吧!和巴尔底人[178]打仗,对于你的昵友呢,则需要和平、诙谐和一切能激发爱情的东西。

Ⅳ: Be Patient and Comply

If she's not charming or courteous enough, at your loving, endure it and persist: she'll soon be kinder. You can get a curved branch to bend on the tree by patience: you'll break it, if you try out your full strength. With patience you can cross the water: you'll not conquer the river by sailing against the flow. Patience tames tigers and Numidian lions: the farmer in time bows the ox to the plough. Who was fiercer than Arcadian Atalanta? Wild as she was she still surrendered to male kindness. Often Milanion wept among the trees at his plight and at the girl's harsh acts: often at her orders his shoulders carried the nets, often he pierced wild boars with his deadly spear: and he felt the pain of Hylaeus's tense bow; but that of another bow was still more familiar. I don't order you to climb in Maenalian woods, holding a weapon, or carrying nets on your back: I

4.忍耐与服从

假如你的情妇很难服侍而且对你也不仁慈，那么你就必须耐着性子忍受着；她不久就会柔和下来的。假如你小心翼翼地拗一根树枝，它就会弯曲，假如你拿起来用力一拗，那它就会断了。小心地顺着水流，人们就可以游过一条河；可是假如你逆着水性，你就总也不能到达目的地。人们用忍耐驯服了纳米第阿[179]的老虎和狮子；在田里的雄牛也渐渐屈服于犁耙了。还有比诺那克里阿人阿达朗达[180]更厉害的女子吗？但是随便她如何骄傲，她终究还是被一个男子[181]的柔情所调理。别人说，米拉尼洪时常在树林里为自己的命运和那少女[182]的严厉而痛哭。他时常遵从她的命令把捕捉禽兽用的网负在自己身上，时常用他的长矛去刺那可怕的野猪。他甚至中了希拉葛思[183]的箭；可是其他的箭[184]他也是受过的啊！我并没有命令你手里拿着兵器到梅拿鲁思山[185]的森林中去，也不命令你把沉重

don't order you to bare your chest to flying darts; the tender commands of my arts are safe.

Yield to opposition: by yielding you'll end as victor; Only play the part she commands you to. Condemn what she condemns: what she approves, approve; say what she says; deny what she denies. She laughs, you laugh; remember to cry, if she cries; she'll set the rules according to your expression. If she plays, tossing the ivory dice in her hand, throw

阿尔迦第阿国王阿达朗达

的网背在肩上;我更不能命令你去袒胸受箭。聪明人,我的课程将教给你最容易学的命令。

假如你的情人不依你,那么你就要让步:让步之后才会获得胜利。不论她叫你去做什么事情,你都要为她做好。她所骂的,你也骂;她所称赞的,你也称赞;她要说的,你也跟着说;她所否认的,你也否认;她如果笑,你就陪着她笑;如果她哭,那你也少不了要流泪:一言以蔽之,你要照着她的脸色来确定你自己的脸色。她喜欢赌博,她的手掷着象牙骰子,你

them wrong, and concede on your bad throw; If you play knucklebones, no prize if you win, make out that often the ruinous low Dogs fell to you. And if it's draughts, the draughtsmen mercenaries, let your champion be swept away by your glass foe. Yourself, hold your girl's sunshade outspread, yourself, make a place for her in the crowd. Quickly bring up a footstool to her elegant couch, and slip the sandal on or off her sweet foot. Often, even though you're shivering yourself, her hand must be warmed at your neglected breast. Don't think it shameful (though it's shameful, you'll like it), to hold the mirror for her in your noble hands. When his stepmother, Juno, was tired of sending him monsters, Hercules, it's said, who reached the heavens he'd shouldered,

海尔古赖斯

呢，要故意掷得不好，然后把骰子递给她。假如玩小骰子游戏，为了不使她因为失败而悲伤，你就应当让她赢。假如棋盘是你们的战场，那你的玻璃棋子也就应当被你的敌手打败。你需要为她打着遮阳伞；假如她挤在人群中，你便要为她开路；你要匆匆走到跳脚板的边上去扶她上舁床，将鞋子从她的纤足脱下或者是穿上。有的时候即使你自己很冷，你也要把你情妇冰冷的手在你的怀里捂暖。用你的手、自由人的手，去为她拿着镜子，这虽然有点儿不好意思，但是绝对不要害羞。那个使母亲不愿意把怪物放在他路上的神祇[186]，注定要

held a basket, among the Lydian girls, and spun raw wool. The hero of Tiryns complied with his girl's orders: go now, and endure the misgivings he endured. Ordered to appear in town, make sure you arrive before time, and don't leave unless it's late. She tells you to be elsewhere: drop everything, run, don't let the crowd in the way stop you trying. She's returning home from another party at night: when she calls for her slave you come too. She's in the country, says: "come"; Love hates a laggard; if you've no wheels, travel the road on foot. Don't let bad weather, or parching Dog-days, stall you, or the roads whitened by falling snow.

进他起初背叛过神祇的天堂，据说曾经在伊奥尼阿的处女们中间拿过女红的篮子还纺过羊毛。谛伦斯的英雄[187]都服从他昵友的命令。你现在不要踌躇，快去忍受他所忍受的情况吧！假如她约你到市场去相会，你必须常常在约定的时间之前很早就等在那儿，而回来的时间则是越迟越好。她对你说："你到某个地方来。"你就要将一切事情都放弃跑过去，不要让别人延迟了你的步履。晚上，当她从华筵里出来，喊一个奴隶领路回去的时候，你要立刻上去自荐。她在乡间写信告诉你："请您惠临。"阿谟尔是憎恨迟缓的；没有车，你就立刻抬起脚来上路。什么都不能阻拦你，天气不好也不要管，炙热的夏天也不要管，大雪纷飞也不要管。

Ⅴ：Don’t be Faint-Hearted

Love is a kind of warfare. Slackers，dismiss！There are no cowards guarding this standard. Night and winter，long roads and cruel sorrows，and every kind of labour are found on love’s campaigns. You’ll often endure rain pouring from heavenly clouds，and frozen，lie there on the naked earth. They say that Phoebus grazed Admetus’s cattle，and found shelter in a humble hut. Who can’t suit what suited Phoebus? Lose your pride，you who’d have love’s sorrows tamed. If you’re denied a safe and

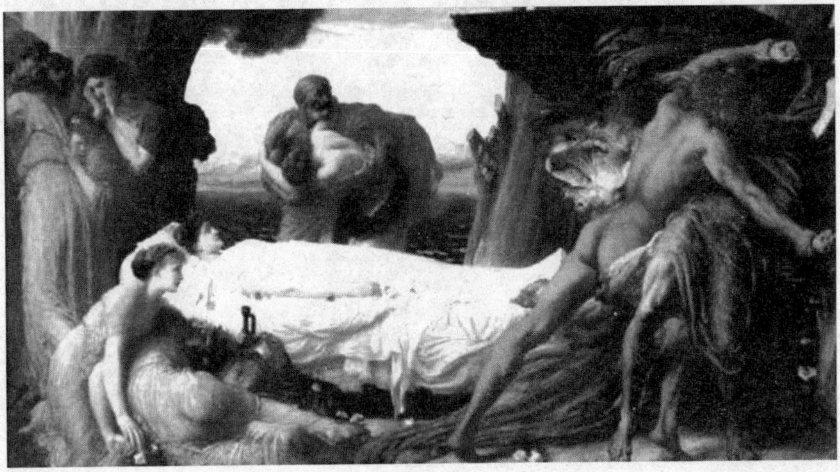

阿特美都思

5.不要胆怯

爱情就像在军中服役。懦怯的人们，退后吧！懦夫是不配保护这些旗帜的。幽夜、寒冬、远路、辛苦、烦恼，这全都是在这快乐的战场上所需要忍受的。你需要时常忍受那云彩注在你身上的雨水，你也需要时常忍受寒冷，伏地而睡。有人说，肯丢斯的神衹[188]费雷的王在放牧阿特美都思[189]的牛时，他只有一间小茅舍作为栖身之所。斐菩斯[190]都不会害羞的事情谁会当做可耻呢？去掉一切的骄傲，假如你想要恋爱得长久。假如你没有

level road, and the door barred with a bolt against you, then drop down head–first through the open roof: a high window too offers a secret way. She'll be glad, knowing the chase itself is risky for you: that will be sure proof to the lady of your love. You might often have been parted from your girl, Leander: you swam across so she could know your heart.

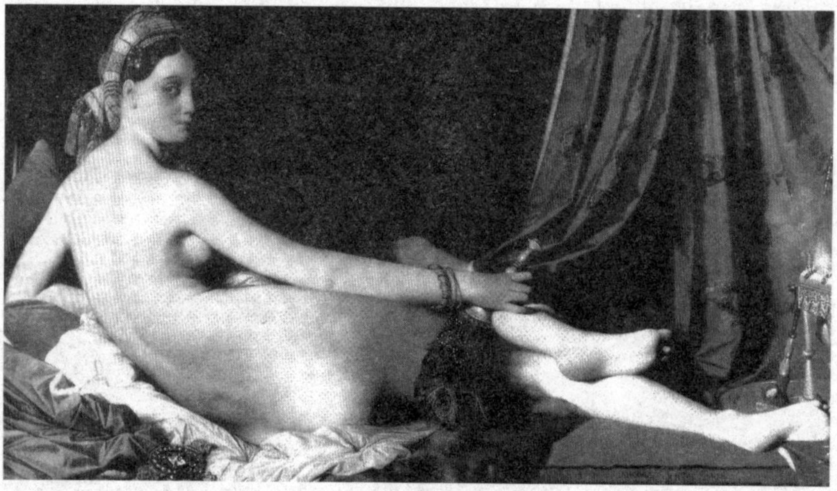

神祇的情妇

一条安全又方便的路去会你的情妇，假如门关得紧紧的不能使你进去，好，你就爬上屋顶，从这条危险的路到你的情人那儿去；或者是从高窗上溜进去也可以。她如果知道了你冒险的原因，一定会非常高兴的，这样你的爱情也就有了确切的保证。莱盎德罗斯[191]啊，你可以不必常常去看你的情人！你乘风破浪游过大海，向她证明你对她的感情。

Ⅵ: Win Over the Servants

Nor is it shameful to you to cultivate her maids, according to their grades, and the serving men. Greet them by their names (it costs you nothing) clasp humble hands with yours, in your ambition. And even offer the servant, who asks, a little something on Fortune's Day (it's little enough to pay); and the maid, on that day when the hand of punishment fell on the Gauls, they deluded by maids in mistress's clothes. Trust me, make the people yours: especially the gatekeeper, and whoever lies in front of her bedroom doors.

幸运之神

6.赢得仆人的心

不应当以和侍女、女佣、奴隶结交为可耻。向她们一一致敬，这对于你来说是没有什么损害的。你要去握她们卑微的手。而且，在富尔都拿的日子[192]，你还得送一些小礼物给那些向你乞讨的奴隶，这些花费对于你来说是非常有限的。而在那迦里阿人受了罗马侍女们衣饰的欺骗而丧生的日子[193]，也要送一点礼物给侍女。相信我，把这些小人物都搜罗在你自己的利益中。不要忘了那守门人，和看守卧房门的奴隶。

Ⅶ：Give Her Little Tasteful Gifts

I don't tell you to give your mistress expensive gifts：give little but of that little，skilfully，give what's fitting. When the field is full of riches，when the branches bend with the weight，let the boy bring a gift in a rustic basket. You can say it was sent from your country villa，even though it was bought on the Via Sacra. Send grapes，or those nuts Amaryllis loved，chestnuts，but she doesn't love them now. Why even thrushes are fine，and the gift of a dove，to witness your remembrance of your mistress. Shameful to send them hoping for the death of some childless old man. Ah，perish those who make giving a crime! Do I also teach that you send tender verses? Ah me，poems are not honoured much. Songs are praised，but its gifts they really want：barbarians themselves are pleasing，so long as they're rich. Truly now it is the Age of Gold：the greatest honours come with gold：love's won by gold. Even if you came，Homer，with the Muses

7.给她一些小礼物

我也并不是叫你拿华美的礼物去送给你的情妇：送她些不值什么钱的东西，只要是精选的而且送得适宜就可以了。在田野铺陈着它的富庶时，当果树挂着累累果实的时候，差一个奴隶送满满一篮子的乡村礼物给她。虽然果子不过是从圣路[194]上买来的，你却可以对她说是从乡间采来的。送她一些葡萄或者是阿马里力思[195]所爱吃的栗子；可是今天的阿马里力思不很爱吃栗子了[196]。你甚至还可以送她一只画眉鸟或者是一个花鬘，表示你是在思念着她。我知道别人也曾经买过这些东西去送给没有儿女的老人，冀望在他死后能够得到他的遗产。啊！用这些礼物来做那种不怀好意用途的人简直该死！我劝你赠她几首情诗吧。啊！诗词并不是体面的。她们赞美诗词，但是她们所要的却是贵重的礼物，只要有钱，即使是一个粗人也可以得到人们的欢心。我们的时代是真正的黄金时

as companions, if you brought nothing with you, Homer, you'd be out. Still there are cultured girls, the rarest set; and another set who aren't, but would like to be. Praise either in song; and they'll commend the reader whatever his voice's sweetness: So sing your midnight song to one and the other, perhaps it will figure as a trifling gift.Then what you're about to do, and think is useful, always get your lover to ask you to do it. You promised liberty to one of your slaves: still let him seek the fact of it from your girl; if you stay a punishment, forgo the use of cruel chains, let her be thankful to you, for what you did; the advantage is yours; the title "giver" is your lover's: you lose nothing, she plays the mistress's part.

缪赛女神

代:黄金,让我们得到最大的荣誉;黄金,使我们的恋爱顺利。是的,荷马啊,即使你和九位缪赛一起来,如果你双手空空一无所有的话,荷马啊,别人准会把你赶出门的。虽然有学问的女子并不是没有,可是毕竟是少数,其他的女子却是什么也不懂的,却还要假装知识渊博。可是如果你做起诗来,那么二者就都需要称颂。而你的诗,不管它好还是不好,总要说得中听,使人觉得是有价值的。不论她们是有学问的或者是没有学问的,那首费了一夜时间,连觉都没有睡而为她们做的诗,对她们来说总是可以起一点儿小礼物的作用吧!尤其是当你决定去做一些你认为有用的事情时,你总要想方设法引你的情妇来请求你去做。假如你要把自由给予你的奴隶,你就应当让她来请求你给予他;假如你要赦免一个应当受刑罚的奴隶,也要让她请求你去做。你既可以得到实惠,面子也给了她:你是一点儿损失也没有的,而她却自以为对你很有权威了。

Ⅷ：Favour Her and Compliment Her

But whoever you are，who want to keep your girl，she must think that you're inspired by her beauty. If she's dressed in Tyrian robes，praise Tyrian：if she's in Coan silk，consider Coan fitting. She's in gold-thread? She's more precious than gold：She wears wool，approve the wool she's wearing. She leaves off her tunic，cry："You set me on fire"，but request her anxiously to beware of chills. She's parted her hair：praise the parting：she waves her hair；be pleased with the waves. Admire her limbs as she dances，her voice when she sings，and when it finishes，grieve that it's finished in words. It's fine if you tell her what delights，and what gives joy about her lovemaking，her skill in bed. Though she's more violent than fierce Medusa，she'll be "kind and gentle" to her lover. But make sure of this：don't let your expression give your speech the lie，lest

8.赞美她、支持她

可是假如你存心要保持你和情妇的爱情，你就必须做出使她相信你是在欣赏她的美貌的样子。她披着一袭帝路司[197]的绛色大氅，你就要称赞那帝路司的绛色大氅。她穿着一件高司[198]的织物，你就要说高司的织物她穿起来最般配。她佩戴闪耀的金饰，你便对她说在你看来黄金还比不上她的娇容灿烂。假如她穿着贵重的裘衣，你就要称赞那件裘衣；假如她穿着一件单衫，你就应当高呼起来——"你让我的眼睛都看花了"，还要低微地请求她当心不要冻坏了身子。假如她的发丝是艺术地在额前分开，你就要称赞这种梳理的方法；假如她的头发是用热烙铁卷过的，你就应该说："好美丽的卷发！"在她跳舞的时候，你要赞叹她的手臂；在她唱歌的时候，你要赞叹她的声音；而当她停歇的时候，你还要充满失望地说结束得太快了。等到她允许你和她同睡之后，你便可以崇拜那使你幸福

you seem a deceiver with words. Art works when its hidden: discovery brings shame, and time destroys faith in everything of merit.

魔女梅度沙

的东西了，你更可以用一种快乐得有些战栗的声音表示出你的狂欢来。是的，即使她比可怕的梅度沙[199]还凶，她也会为她的情郎变得温柔而容易驯服。你尤其应当善于矫饰，使她不能够察觉，而你的脸色千万不可露出你的言语，艺术的隐藏是有用的。显露出来便成为羞耻，而且会永远失去别人的信任。

Ⅸ：Comfort Her in Sickness

Often in autumn, when the season's loveliest, and the ripe grape's dyed with purple juice, when now we're frozen solid, now drenched with heat, the body's listless in the changing air. Your girl's well in fact; but if she's lying sick, feels ill because of the unhealthy weather, then let love and devotion be obvious to your girl, then sow what you'll reap later with full sickle. Don't be put off by the fretfulness of the patient, let yours be the

病中的美女

9.让病中的她感到安慰

在一般情况下，快到秋天的时候，那时正是一年中最好的时节，那时葡萄累累地垂着，那时我们时常可以感到一阵透骨的新寒，有时感到一阵炙人的炎热，这种天气是很容易使我们疲倦的。希望你的情妇那时很健康！可是假如她有些微恙而被牵制在床上，假如她受天气不好的影响而生病，那将是展示你对爱情忠诚的时候了；那就是应当播种获得一个

hand that does what she allows. And be seen weeping, and don't shrink from kisses, let her parched mouth drink from your tears. Pray a lot, but all aloud; and, as often as she lets you, tell her happy dreams that you remembered. And let the old woman come who cleanses room and bed, bringing sulphur and eggs in her trembling hands. The signs of a welcome devotion are in all this: by these means into wills many have made their way. But don't let dislike for your attentions rise from illness, only be charming, in your earnestness: don't prohibit food, or hand her cups of bitter stuff: let your rival mix all that for her.

爱的呵护

丰收的时候了。你要不怕烦琐地去侍候病中的她;你的手要去做一切她吩咐的事;要让她看见你哭泣;不要不和她接吻,要让她枯干的嘴唇饮着你的眼泪!为她的健康许愿,应答尤其要大声;而且要时常预备一些预示吉兆的梦对她讲。叫一个老妇人拿着硫矿和赎罪的蛋去清洁她的床:在她的心里,这些举动会永远成为她一个温柔的记忆。多少人用这种方法从遗嘱上得到一个地位啊!可是要当心,过分地讨好是会让病人讨厌的:你多情的举动需要有一个限制。制止她吃零食和请她吃苦药这样的事你是不应当去做的!这些事让你的敌人去做吧!

Ⅹ: Let Her Miss You: But Not For Long

But the winds that filled your sails and blew offshore, are no use when you're in the open sea. While young love's wandering, it gathers strength by use: if you nourish it well, it will be strong in time. The bull you fear's the calf you used to stroke: the tree you lie beneath was a sapling; the river's tiny when born, but gathers riches in its flow, and collects the many waters that come to it. Make her accustomed to you: nothing's greater than habit; while you're captivating her, avoid no boredom. Let her always be seeing you: always giving you ear; show your face, at night and in the day. When you've more confidence that you'll be missed, when your absence far away will cause her worry, give her a rest: the fields when rested repay the loan, and parched earth drinks the heavenly rain. Phyllis burnt less for Demophoon in his presence: she

10.让她想念你,但不要太久

可是当你离开港口的时候,风不一定就是你航行在大海中所需要的风。爱情在初生的时候是微弱的;它将因为习惯而坚强起来;你需要好好养育它,它便会慢慢地坚强起来。这头让你现在感到畏惧的雄牛,在它小的时候你曾经抚摸过;这株你高卧在它绿荫下的大树,起初不过是一根小小的枝儿。江河是涓涓溪流汇集而成的。设法让你的美人和你熟稔,因为唯有习惯是最有力量的。为了能够得到她的心,千万不要在任何敌人面前退却。要让她不断地看见你,要让她不断地听见你的声音。不论白天黑夜,你必须常常在她的眼前。可是当你坚信她能够念念不忘你的时候,你就要离开她,要使你的离别带给她一些牵挂。给她一些休息,一片休息过的田地种起来才会更加丰盛,一片干燥的土壤吸收雨水才会更加猛烈。当岱莫冯[200]在菲丽丝[201]身旁的时候爱情是并不十分热烈的;但是当

blazed more fiercely when he sailed away. Penelope was tormented by the loss of cunning Ulysses: you, Laodamia, by absent Protesilaus. But brief delays are best: fondness fades with time, love vanishes with absence, and new love appears. When Menelaus left, Helen did not lie alone, Paris, the guest, at night, was taken to her warm breast. What craziness was that, Menelaus? You left wife and guest alone under the same roof. Madman, would you trust timid doves to a hawk? Would you trust the full fold to a mountain wolf? Helen did not sin: her lover committed none: what you, what anyone would do, he did. You forced adtery by giving time and place: What did the girl employ but your

脱拉岂阿国王的女儿菲丽丝

他航海远行后，她爱情的火焰却猛烈得燃烧起来了。珮耐洛泊[202]因为聪敏的屋里赛思[203]的别离而痛苦;而你的眼泪，拉奥达米阿[204]啊，将那费拉古思的孙子[205]喊回来。可是，为了谨慎起见，你的别离最好还是短一些为妙:时间会减弱牵挂的心。长久看不见的情郎是很容易被遗忘的:别人将会取而代之。美奈拉乌思不在家的时候，海伦无法忍受孤眠的滋味，便到她宾客[206]的怀中去温存了。美奈拉乌思，你是多么傻啊！你独自走了，把你的妻子和你的宾客放在一个屋子里。傻子！这简直就是把温柔的鸽子放在老鹰的爪子里，把柔弱的羊托付给饥饿的狼！不，海伦是没有罪的，她的情夫也是没有罪的。他做了你

counsel? What should she do? Her man away, a cultivated guest, and she afraid to sleep alone in an empty bed. Let Atrides appear: I acquit Helen of crime: she took advantage of her husband's courtesy.

岱莫冯

自己或者是随便哪一个人都可以做的事。那是你强迫他们通奸的,为他们提供了时间和地点, 这难道不就如同是你让你年轻的妻子这样做的吗?她做了什么呢?她的丈夫不在家,在她旁边的是一个并不粗鲁愚蠢的宾客,而且她又是害怕孤独的。请阿特拉思的儿子[207]想一想他要怎样吧:我是能够宽恕海伦的,她不过是利用了一个多情丈夫的殷勤而已。

Ⅺ: Have Other Friends: But Be Careful

But the red-haired boar is not so fierce in mid-anger. When he turns and threatens the rabid pack, or the lioness giving suck to unweaned cubs, or the tiny viper crushed by a careless foot, as a woman when a rival's caught in her lover's bed: she blazes, her face the colour of her heart. She storms with fire and flame, all restraint forgot, as if struck, as they say, by the horns of the Boeotian god. Wronged by her husband, her marriage violated, savage Medea avenged herself through her children. Another fatal mother was that swallow, you see there: look, her breast carries the stain of blood. Well-founded and firm loves have been dissolved so: these are crimes to make cautious men afraid. Not that my censure condemns you to only one girl: the gods forbid! A wife could hardly expect that. Indulge, but secretly veil your sins, with restraint: it's no glory to

11.交其他女友:但要小心谨慎

可是那被猎人的猎犬追赶的狂怒的野猪,那正在给小狮子哺乳的牝狮,那旅人不小心踏到的蝮蛇,都没有一个在丈夫的床上捉住情敌的女子那样可怕。她的狂怒显现在她的脸上:铁器、火,在她看来一切都是好的;她忘记了一切节制,她奔跑着,像被阿沃尼亚神祇的角[208]所触动的跳神女子一样。丈夫的罪恶,结发夫妻的背誓,一个生在法西斯河畔的野蛮妻子在她自己的儿子身上实施了报复[209]。另一个丧失了本性的母亲,就是这只你所看见的燕子。你看着它,它的胸口还染着鲜血。那最适当的配偶,最坚固的关系就是这样断裂的:一个聪明的男子是不应当去煽起这种妒忌的暴怒的。严厉的批评者啊,我并没有判定你只准有一个情妇。天保佑我!一个已经结婚的女子是很难遵守这种约束的。娱乐着吧,可是必须谨慎;你多情的偷吃需要隐藏起来,而不应该夸耀出来。不要拿一件其

you to be seeking out wrongdoing. Don't give gifts another girl could spot, or have set times for your assignations. And lest a girl catch you out in your favourite hauntsdon't meet all of them in one place. And always look closely at your wax tablets, whenever you write: lest much more is read there than you sent. Wounded, Venus takes up just arms, and hurls her dart, and makes you lament, as she is lamenting. While Agamemnon was satisfied with one woman, Clytemnestra was chaste: evil was done through the man's fault. She had heard how Chryses, with sacred head-bands, and laurel in his hand, failed to win back his daughter: she had heard of your sorrows, captive Briseis, and how scandalous delays had prolonged the war. She heard all

赛伊斯

他女子能够认得出来的礼物送给这个女子；改变你们幽会的地点和时间，不要使一个女子知道你的秘密来揭穿你。当你写信的时候，在没有寄出之前必须细细地重新看一遍：许多妇人都能够看得出弦外之音。被冒犯的维纳斯拿起了武器，来一箭，再来一箭，使那放箭的人也感到苦痛。当阿特拉思的儿子[210]对他的妻子[211]感到满意时，她是贞洁的；她丈夫的薄幸使她犯了罪。她知道那个手里拿着月桂冠，额上缠着圣带的克里赛司[212]不能收回自己的女儿。她知道了，利尔奈索斯的女子[213]，引起你的痛苦又经过可耻的延迟而延长了战争的劫掠[214]。这些她不过都是耳闻罢了，可是那泊里阿摩思的女儿[215]，她是亲眼看见的，因为，真可耻，那个胜利者反倒做了他俘虏的俘虏了。从此那登达勒思的女儿[216]就让谛爱斯带思的儿子[217]投到了她的心中，投到了她的床

this; she saw Cassandra for herself: the victor the shameful prize of his own prize. Then she took Thyestes to her heart and bed, and wrongfully avenged the Atrides's crime.

Even if the acts, you've well hidden, become known, though they're known, still always deny them. Don't be subdued, or more fond than usual: those are the signs of many guilty thoughts. But don't forgo sex: all peace is in that one thing. The act it is that disproves a prior union.

泊里阿摩思的女儿珈桑特拉

上，她用一种罪恶去报复她丈夫的罪恶。

你的行为，虽然隐藏得很好，但是如果一旦暴露出来，或者被发觉了，你一定要否认到底。不要比平常更卑屈更谄媚：因为这就是做贼心虚的表现。你需要用尽平生之力，用对于情战全盘的精力；和平是只有这样才能够换到的：是应当让床榻来证明你以前没有偷尝过维纳斯的幽欢。

Ⅻ: Aphrodisiacs?

There are those who prescribe eating a dish of savory, a noxious herb, my judgement is its poisonous; or mix pepper with the seeds of stinging nettles; or crush yellow camomile in well-aged wine. But the goddess who holds high Eryx, beneath the shaded hill, doesn't force you to suffer like this for her delights. White onions brought from Megara, Alcathous's city, and rocket, herba salax, the kind that comes from gardens, eat those, and eggs, eat honey from Hymettus, and seeds from the cones of sharp-neededled pines.

维纳斯女神

12.春药?

有些老妇人劝你用玉帚那种恶草，或者是胡椒掺入刺激的荨麻子，或者是黄色除虫菊浸泡陈酒来做兴奋剂，在我看来，这些简直就是毒药。那住在艾里克斯山[218]幽荫山风中的女神，是不愿意用这些人工的方法来激起她的欢乐的。那你可以用的，是从希腊阿尔加都思[219]城运到我们这里的白胡葱，或者是生在我们园子里的动情草，或者是鸡蛋，或者是希买多斯[220]的蜜，或者是松球包着的松子。

XⅢ: Stir her Jealousy

Wise Erato, why turn to magic arts? My chariot's scraping the inside post. You who just hid your crimes on my advice, change course, and on my advice reveal your secrets. I'm not guilty of fickleness: the curved prow is not always blown onwards by the same wind. Now we run to a Thracian northerly, an easterly now, sometimes a west wind fills our sails, sometimes a south. Look how the charioteer now slacks the reins, then skilfully restrains the galloping team. There are those who don't like being served with shy kindness: while love fades if there's no rival around. Generally heads are swollen with success, it's not easy to be content with the good times. As a fire with little power, gradually consumed, hides itself, ashes whitening on its surface, but the doused flames will flare with a pinch of sulphur, and the brightness, that was there before, returns: so

13.燃起她的妒火

可是多才的爱拉陀，你为什么使我在这些邪术中迷失呢？回到我的车子所不应该越出的正路吧！刚才我劝你隐藏你的薄幸！现在我却劝你换一条路走，发表你的薄幸。不要骂我自相矛盾，并不是每阵风都适宜行船的；它航行在波涛之上，有时被从脱拉岂阿来的鲍雷阿思[221]推动着，有时被曷虑斯[222]推动着；宙费路思[223]和诺多思[224]轮流吹拂着它的帆，你看那驾车的人吧：有时他放松了缰绳，有时他勒住了狂奔的马。有些女子是不喜欢懦弱和顺从的，没有一个情敌，她们的爱情就会歇散下去。幸福时常使我们沉醉，但是人们却很难长久地享受它。火没有了燃料便会渐渐地熄灭，消失在白白的灰烬下面；可是一撒上硫矿，那好像已经沉睡的火便又重新燃烧起来而且释放出一道新的光芒。因此，假如一颗心憔悴在一种无知觉的麻痹中，你便应该用嫉妒的针去刺激它让它醒来。你必须

when hearts are numbed by slack dullness and security, love is aroused by some sharp stimulus. Make her fearful for you: warm her tepid mind; let her grow pale at evidence of your guilt. Oh four times happy, times impossible to count, is he for whom his wounded girl grieves.

That, when his sins reach her unwilling ears, she's lost, and voice and colour flee the unhappy girl. Let me be him, whose hair the angry woman tears: let me be him, whose tender cheeks nails seek, him whom she sees with tears, turns on him tortured eyes, whom though she can't live without, she wishes she could. If you ask how long you should let her lament her hurt, keep it brief, lest a long delay kindles anger's force:

医药神之子马卡翁

让你的情妇因为你而不得安宁,唤醒她心头冷却的热焰,让她在知道你的薄幸时脸儿发青。哦,哪有一个自觉受了欺凌而啜泣着的情妇还会感到一百倍甚至一千倍的幸福啊!她不愿意怀疑他犯罪,但是当他犯罪的消息一传到她耳边,她就晕过去了,多么不幸的女子啊!她的脸和声音都变了。我是多么愿意做那被她在暴怒中拔着头发的人啊!我是多么愿意做那被她用手指甲抓破脸又使她看了落泪的人啊!她愤怒地看着这个人,没有了他,她是不能活的,但是她是愿意活的!可是你要问我了,我应

throw your arms straightaway around her snow-white neck, and let the weeping girl fall on your chest. Kiss her who weeps, make sweet love to her who weeps, there'll be peace: this is the one way anger's dissolved. When she's truly raging, when she seems fixed on war, then sue for peace in bed, she'll be gentle. There Harmony dwells with grounded arms: there, trust me, is the place where grace is born. Doves that once fought, now bill and coo, whose murmur is of caressing words. At first all things were confused mass without form, heaven and earth and sea were created one: soon sky was set above land, earth circled by water, and random chaos split into its parts. Forests allowed the creatures a home: air the birds; fish took shelter in the running streams. Then the human race wandered the empty wilds, a thing of naked strength and brutish body: woods were its home, grass its food, leaves its bed; and for a long time no man knew another. They say sweet delights softened savage spirits: when man and woman rested in one place: they had no teacher to show

当让她失望多久呢?我将回答你:时间不可太长,否则她的怒气就会更加有力了。赶快用你的手臂缠住她的玉颈,将她涕泪淋漓的脸儿紧贴在你的胸口。把甜蜜的吻给予她的眼泪,将维纳斯的幽欢给予她的眼泪。这样便相安无事了:这是让她息怒的唯一方法。可是当她怒不可遏的时候,当她对你不肯善罢干休的时候,你就请求她在床上签订和平公约;她便会柔和下去了。想要不用武力就可以平静地处在和议厅中就是这样的;相信我,宽恕是从那个地方产生出来的。那些刚才还互相争斗的鸽子亲起嘴来是格外有情的,而它们的鸣叫是一种爱情的语言。宇宙起初不过只是一团混沌,也没有划分出天、地和水,不久天升到了地的上面,而海又环绕着陆地,空虚的混沌就变成了各种原形。树林成为了野兽的居所,空间成了飞鸟的家乡,游鱼潜藏在水里。那时人类孤寂地漂泊在田野中间,他们只是有力而无智的,只是一个粗蛮的身体。他们以树林为屋,以野草为食,以树叶为床;他们很长时间都互相不认识。别人说,男子和女子合在一张床上温柔的逸乐柔化了他们的蛮性。他们要做的事情,他们单独

them what to do, Venus did her work without sweet art. Birds have mates to love: in the midst of watersa fish will find another to share her joy; hind follows stag, snake will bind with snake, bitch clings entwined with some adulterous dog; ewes delight in being covered; bulls delight in heifers, too, the snub-nosed she-goat supports her rank mate. Mares driven to frenzy follow their stallion, through distant places beyond the branching river. So act, and offer strong medicine to your angry one: only this will bring peace to her unhappiness; this medicine beats Machaon's drugs: this will reinstate you when you've sinned.

艾思古拉比乌思

自习就会了，也不用请教先生：维纳斯也不用艺术帮忙，竟完成了她温柔的公干。鸟儿有它所爱的牝鸟；鱼儿在水中找到一个伴儿来平分它的欢乐。雌鹿跟随着雄鹿；蛇和蛇合在了一起；雄狗和雌狗配对；母羊和母牛沉醉在公羊和雄牛的抚爱中；那雄山羊，不管它是如何的不洁，也不会使淫逸的雌山羊扫兴。沉浸在爱情狂热中的牝马，甚至会越过河流到远处去寻找雄马。勇敢啊！用这些强有力的药去平息你情妇的愤怒；这种药能够使她在深切的苦痛沉睡过去，这比马卡翁[225]一切的液汁都灵验，假如你有了过失，只有它才能够使你得到宽恕。

XⅣ: Be Wise and Suffer

While I was writing this, Apollo suddenly appeared plucking the strings of his lyre with his thumb. Laurel was in his hand, laurel wreathing his hair: he appears to poets looking like that. "Professor of Wanton Love," he said to me, "go lead your disciples to my temple, it's where the famous words, celebrated throughout the world, command everyone to 'Know Yourself'. He alone will be wise, who's well-known to himself, and carries out each work that suits his powers. Whom nature's given beauty, let it be seen by her: whose skin is lustrous, lie there often with

太阳神阿波罗

14.要明智与忍耐

当我写到这里的时候，忽然阿波罗现身在我前面；他用手指拨弄着他的金琴。一枝月桂在他的手中，一顶月桂冠戴在他的头上。他用一种先知的态度和口气对我说："放逸爱情的大师，快把你的弟子们领到我的殿中来吧！他们在那里可以念那全世界闻名的铭：'凡人，认识你自己。'[226]只有认识自己的人在爱情中才会聪明，只有他才会量力而行。假如老天赐予他一副俊俏的脸，他应该知道如何去利用它，假如他有一身好的皮肤，他就得时常袒怀而卧，假如他话说得很漂亮，就不可能默默无语一声不响。他如果擅长歌唱，就应该唱；如果善饮，就应该饮。可是

bare shoulders; who delights by talking, avoid taciturn silence; who sings with art, then sing; who drinks with art, then drink. but the eloquent should never declaim midspeech nor the crazy poet ever read his poems!" So Phoebus warned: take note of Phoebus's warning; truth's surely on the sacred lips of that god.

To bring us back to earth: who loves wisely wins, and by my skill will bring off what he seeks. It's not often the furrow repays the loan with interest, not often the winds aid the boat in trouble: What delights a lover is little, what pains him more; many sufferings declare themselves to his heart. As many as hares on Athos, the bees that graze on Hybla, as many as the olives the grey-green branches carry, or the sea-shells on the shore, are the pains of love: the

斐菩斯

烦琐的演说家和怪癖的诗人啊，千万不要朗诵你们的散文或者诗来打断谈话。"斐菩斯的教导是这样的。有情的人们啊，服从斐菩斯的高论吧！你们可以完全相信这从神明的口中发出来的言语。可是我的题旨在呼唤我了。凡是谨慎地爱着又听从我的艺术教条的人，一定会胜利达到他的目的。

田地不是经常都有好收成的，风也不是经常帮助驾舟的人。欢乐很少而悲痛却很多，这就是多情男子们的命运，愿他准备着让灵魂受千万次的折磨吧！阿笃斯山[227]上的兔子，希勃拉山[228]上的蜜蜂，荫密的葩拉丝

thorns we suffer from are drenched in gall. They'll say she's gone out: very likely she's to be seen inside: think that she has gone out, and your vision lied. The door will be shut the night she promised you: endure it, lay your body on the dusty ground. And perhaps the lying maid with scornful face, will say: "Why's he hanging round our door?" Still, a suppliant, coax the doorposts, and your harsh mistress, and hang the roses, from your head, outside. Come if she wishes: when she shuns you, go; it's unbecoming to a noble man to bore her. Why let your lover say: "There's no escaping him"? Her feelings won't always be against you. Don't think it a disgrace to suffer curses or blows from the girl, or plant kisses on her tender feet.

树[229]上的珠果，海滩上的贝壳，这些比起恋爱的痛苦来说真是少极了。我们所中的箭上面满蘸着苦胆。当你看见你的情妇在家的时候，她们却会对你说她已经出去了。这有什么关系呢，就算她已经出去了，就当你的眼睛看错就是了。她允许你在夜间和她相见，而到了夜间她的门却关得紧紧的，忍受着，睡在肮脏的地上。或许有一个撒谎的侍女前来，粗蛮地对你说："这人为什么站在我们的门前？"那时你就应当恳求这个侍女，甚至是那闭着的门，把头上的蔷薇[230]放在门槛上[231]。假如你的情妇愿意见你了，你便跑进去，假如她拒绝了你，你就走吧，一个有教养的人不应该成为让人憎恶的人。你难道要你的情妇说"简直没有办法避开这个可厌的人"吗？美人总是喜怒无常的。不要怕羞，要愿意去忍受她的辱骂、挨她的打，或者是去吻她的纤足。

XV: Respect Her Freedom

Why waste time on trifles? Greater themes arise: I sing great things; `pay attention, people. We labour hard, but virtue's nothing if not hard: hard labour's what my art demands. Be patient with your rival, victory rests with you: you'll be victor on Great Jupiter's hill. Believe me, it's no man says this, but Chaonia's sacred oaks: my art contains nothing more profound than this. If she flirts, endure it; if she writes, don't touch the wax; let her come from where she wishes; and go where she pleases, too. This husbands allow their lawfully married wives, when you come, gentle sleep, to play your part, as well. I'm not perfect in this art, I confess: What can I do? I'm less than my own instructions. What, shall I let some man signal openly to my girl, and bear it, and not show anger if I wish? I remember her husband kissed her: I grieved at the kiss he gave; my love's

15.尊重她的自由

可是,我为什么要说到这些琐细的地方呢?我们将注意力放在重要的题目上吧!我要说重大的事项了。老百姓,请当心啊!我的企图是冒险的,可是没有冒险,哪里会有成功?我的功课所要求你的是一件烦难的工作。耐心地忍受着一个情敌,你的凯旋才靠得住,你才可以胜利进入大裘比德的神殿。相信我,这并不是凡夫的俗见,却是希腊橡树[232]的神示,这是我所传授的艺术的无上的教条。假如你的情妇向你的情敌做媚眼、打手势,那么要忍受着。她写信给他,你千万不要去碰她的信。任她自由地来来去去,多少丈夫以这种殷勤对他们的发妻,尤其是当一觉好梦来帮助瞒过他们的时候!至于我,我承认我还不能达到完善的地步。怎么办呢?我还达不到我的艺术。什么!在我眼前,假如有人向我的美人眉眼传情,我便会痛苦得不得了,我忍不住要生气了!我记得有一天她的丈夫和

full of barbarities. Not a few times this fault has hurt me: he's wiser who's reconciled to other mens'coming. But it was better to know nothing: let intrigues be hidden, lest her shameless mouth revealed untruths. How much better, Oh young men, to avoid surprising them: let girls sin, and think, while sinning, that they've fooled you. Love grows with being caught: who are twinned by fortune persist to the end in the cause that ruined them. The story's well known through all the heavens, of Mars and Venus caught by Vulcan's craft. Mars stirred by mad desire for Venus was

爱的自由

她接了一个吻;我便攻击这一吻,我们的爱情充满了无理的要求!而这个女人身上的毛病不知伤害我多少次了。最老练的人是允许别人到他情妇那儿去的。最好是装聋作哑装作什么也不知道。让她掩藏她的不忠,不然长久以后她脸也不会红一红了。年轻的多情人啊,千万不要去揭穿你们的情妇。让她们欺骗你们,让她们在欺骗你们的时候以为你们是被她们的好话所欺骗。揭穿一对情人,那一对情人的爱情反而更深了,等到他们两个利害相关的时候,他们便会坚持到底来补偿他们的损失。有一个故事是整个奥林比阿[233]都知道的,就是胡尔迦奴思[234]用计谋当场拿获马尔

turned from grim warrior to lover. And Venus was not coy or resistant to Mar's pleas (for there's no more loving goddess than her). Ah how often the wanton laughed at her husband's limp, they say, or his hands hardened by his fiery art. She'd openly imitate Vulcan then, to Mars: it became her; great beauty was mingled there with charm. But they used to hide their adultery at first. It was a sin, filled with the blush of shame. The Sun's tale (who can evade the Sun?) made known to Vulcan what his spouse had done. What a poor example, sun, you set! Seek a gift from her, and

胡尔迦奴思

斯和维纳斯的故事。马尔斯神疯狂地爱着维纳斯。这凶猛的战士便变成了一个柔顺的情人。维纳斯对他既不生疏也不残忍；她的心比任何女神都温柔。有人说，那个热恋的女子多少次嘲笑她丈夫的跛行，和他被火或是被工作弄硬的手！同时，她在马尔斯的面前学起胡尔迦奴思的样子：这样在他看来是非常娇媚的，而她讽刺的风姿更使她的美增加千倍。他们起初还只是偷偷摸摸地爱着，他们的热情被掩藏起来而且是害羞的。可是"太阳"(谁能逃过太阳的眼睛呢)却向胡尔迦奴思揭露出他的妻子的行为。你给了一个多么不如意的例子啊，"太

you, if you're quiet, can have what she can give. Vulcan set a hidden net, over and round the bed: it's a piece of work that deceives the eye. Pretends he's off to Lemnos: the lovers come to their assignation: and both lie naked in the net. He calls the gods: the captives are displayed; Venus they think can scarcely restrain her tears. They can't hide their faces, are even unable to cover their sexes with their hands. Then someone laughed

兰诺斯

阳"! 你还不如去向维纳斯请赏。对于你的沉默,她总会给你一些东西作为报答的。胡尔迦奴思在床的四周和上面布上一些穿不透的网罗,这是眼睛所不能看见的,然后他假装动身到兰诺司[235]那里去。这一对情人便来幽会了,于是双双地,赤条条地被捕在网中了。胡尔迦奴思请来诸神,将这一对被捉住的情人给他们看。有人说,维纳斯的眼泪几乎就忍不住了。这两个情人既不能遮他们的脸,又不能用手遮住那不可见人的地方。

and said:“Let me have the chains, Mars, if they're an embarrassment to you!” Their captive bodies are, with difficulty, freed, at your plea, Neptune: Venus runs to Paphos; Mars heads for Thrace. This you achieved, Vulcan: what they hid before, now all shame is gone, they indulge in freely. Now maddened you often confess the thing was foolish, and suffer regret for your cunning. It's forbidden you: Venus once tricked forbids traps to be set, like the one that she endured. Lay out no snares for rivals: don't intercept those secret hand-written messages. Let husbands trap them, if they think they indeed need trapping, husbands to whom the ceremony of fire and water gives the right. Look, I swear again: there's nothing here except what's played within the law; no virtuous woman's caught up in my jests.

那时有一个神衹笑着说了:“诸神中最勇敢的马尔斯,假如铁链弄得你不舒服,就把它们让给我吧！”后来奈泊都诺思请求胡尔迦奴思,他才放了这两个囚犯。马尔斯逃到脱拉岂阿[236]去了。维纳斯逃到巴福斯[237]去了。胡尔迦奴思,这对于你来说有什么好处呢？不久之前他们还掩藏着他们的爱情,现在却公开出来了,因为他们已打破了一切羞耻。你常常承认你的行为是愚笨而鲁莽的,而且别人说你是正在为你自己的谋划而忏悔。我不许你设计陷害他人,那被丈夫当场拿获的第奥奈[238]也禁止你设那种让她曾经受过苦的陷阱。不要布网罗去害你的情敌,不要去盗窃秘密的情书。就是要做,也得让她的正式丈夫去做。至于我,我再重申一遍,我这里所说的只是法律所不禁止的幽欢。我们不要把任何贵妇都混到我们的游戏中来。

XⅥ: Keep It Secret

Who'd dare reveal to the impious the secret rites of Ceres, or uncover the high mysteries of Samothrace? There's little virtue in keeping silent: but speaking of what's kept secret's a heinous crime. O it's good if that babbler Tantalus, clutching at fruit in vain, thirsts in the very middle of the waters! Venus, above all, orders you to be silent about her rites: I warn you, let no idle chatterers come near her. Though the mysteries of Venus are not buried in a box, nor echo in the wide air to the clash of cymbals, but are busily enjoyed so, by us all, they still wish to be concealed among us. Venus, herself, when she takes off her clothes, covers her sex with the half-turned palm of her left hand. Beasts couple indiscriminately in full view: from this sight girls of course turn aside their faces, too. Bedrooms and locked doors suit our intrigues, and shameful

16.保守秘密

谁敢将凯雷丝[239]的圣祭和在刹摩脱拉凯[240]独创的庄严教仪揭露给信教的人看呢?严守秘密是一件微小的功德,反之,说出一件不应当说的事却是一个大大的罪过。不谨慎的唐达鲁思[241]不能取得那悬在他头上的果子,还在水中渴得要死,那简直就是活该。岂带雷阿[242]尤其禁止别人揭穿她的秘密,我警告你,任何多言的人都不准走近她的祭坛。维纳斯的供养并不是藏在柜中的,献祭的时候,钟也不是连连敲着的,我们大家都可以参与,但有一个条件就是大家都必须谨守秘密。即使是维纳斯自己,当她卸下她的衣裳时,她也会用手把她秘密的销魂处遮住。牲畜的交尾是到处都可以看到的,人人都可以看到的,可是少女们,即使已经看见了,也总是避而不看。我们的幽会所不可少的是一间封闭得很严实的房间,而且要把我们不可示人的东西用布遮住。假如我们不要幽暗,至少也要

things are hidden under the sheets: and if not darkness, we seek some veiling shadow, and something less exposed than the light of day. Even back then, when roofs kept out neither rain nor sun, and the oak-tree provided food and shelter, pleasure was had in woods and caves, not under the heavens: such care the native peoples had for their modesty. But now we advertise our nocturnal acts, and nothing's bought if it can't be boasted of! No doubt you'll look out every girl, whatever, to say to whom you please: "She too was mine", and there'll be no lack of those you can point out, so for each that's mentioned there's a shameful tale? Little to cry at: some invent, what they'd deny if true, and claim there isn't one they

农事女神凯雷丝

灰暗或是比白昼暗一些。在那还没有瓦来遮蔽太阳和风雨的时代，在那以橡树来作荫蔽物的时代，多情的人们不是在光天化日之下，而是在山洞里和树林里偷尝爱情的美味；那种野蛮的时代已经开始重视羞耻了！可是现在我们却标榜着我们夜间的功绩，我们以高价换得的是什么呢？把它讲出来是唯一的快乐。而且还到处描述一切女子的爱娇，碰到一个人就说“这个女子我也曾经结识过”，要经常有一个女子可以指点给别人看，要使一切你想染指的女子都成为轻佻的谈话目标。这还不算数：有些人甚至编造出一些故事来(这些故事假如是真的他们一定会否认)，听他们的话，他们是得到了一切女子

haven't slept with. If not their bodies, they touch what they can, their names, and the reputation's gone, though the body's chaste. Odious watchman, go close the girl's door, now, too late, locked with a hundred heavy bars! What's safe, when adulterers give out her name, and want what never happened to be believed? I'm wary even of professing to genuine passions, and, trust me, my secret affairs are wholly hidden.

国王唐达鲁思

眷顾的。假如他们不能接触她们的身体，他们能够损坏她们的名声；身体虽然贞洁，但是名誉却坏了。可憎的守卒，现在就请你滚开吧，把你的情妇关起来，门上还要加着重重的闩锁。对于这些自欺地夸耀着说已得到了她，其实却不能得到幸福的人来说，这些防范又有什么用呢？至于我们呢？我们只含蓄地讲着我们真实的成功；我们的偷香窃玉是受一种不可穿透的缄默的神秘所保护着的。

XⅦ: Don't Mention Her Faults

Above all beware of reproaching girls for their faults, it's useful to ignore so many things. Andromeda's dark complexion was not criticized by Perseus, who was borne aloft by wings on his feet. Andromache by all was rightly thought too tall: Hector was the only one who spoke of her as small. Grow accustomed to what's called bad, you'll call it good. Time heals much: new love feels everything. While a new-grafted twig's growing in the green bark, struck by the lightest breeze, it may fall. Later, hardened by time, it resists the winds, and the strong tree will bear adopted wealth. Time itself erases all faults from the flesh, and what was a flaw, ceases to make you pause. A new oxhide makes nostrils recoil: tamed by familiarity, the odour fades. An evil may be sweetened by its name: let her be "dark" whose pigment's blacker than Illyrian pitch; if she squints, she's like

17.不要提及她的缺点

你尤其不能指责一个女子的坏处:多少情人们都是装聋作哑就过去了!昂德萝美黛[243]脸的颜色,那每只脚上有一只翅膀的人[244]是从来不会进行批评的。盎特罗玛黑[245]的身材大家都认为是很高的:只有一个人以为它是修长合度的,他就是海克笃尔。你所不爱看的就应当试着去看习惯;你就能够很容易接受了;习惯成为自然,而初生的爱情却是什么都会注意到的。在绿色的树皮中孕育的嫩枝,假如微风一吹,它就会折断;可是不久就会和时间牢固地黏在一起,它甚至能够和风对抗,而且结出果子来。时间消磨了一切,即使是那丑陋的体型,我们觉得不完美的,久而久之也就不觉得不完美了。在没有习惯的时候,我们的鼻子是受不了牛皮的气味的,久而久之鼻子闻惯了,也就不觉得讨厌了。而且还有许多字眼儿可以用来掩饰那些坏处。那皮肤比伊里力阿[246]的松脂还要黑的女

Venus; if she's grey, Minerva; let her be "slender", who's truly emaciated: call her "trim", who's tiny, "full-bodied" if she's gross, and hide the fault behind the nearest virtue.

宙斯之子拜尔塞斯

子,你可能说她是浅棕色的。她的眼睛要是斜的呢?你可以把她比作维纳斯[247]。她的眼睛要是黄色的呢?你就说这是米奈尔伐[248]的颜色。那瘦得似乎只有奄奄一息的,你就说是体态轻盈。矮小的就说是娇小玲珑,肥大的就说是盛态丰肌。总而言之,用最相近的语言来掩饰那些坏处。

XⅧ: Don't Ask About Her Age

Don't ask how old she is, or who was Consul when she was born, that's strictly the Censor's duty: Especially if she's past bloom, and the good times gone, and now she plucks the odd grey hair. There's value, Oh youth, in this or a greater age: this will bear seed, this is a field to sow.

体贴的爱人

18.不要问她的年龄

不要问她的年纪,更不要打听她的出身:这些任务都让卫兵去执行吧,尤其是当她已青春不在的时候,良时已过,而她已经在拔她灰白的头发时。青年人啊,这个年龄,或者甚至是更老一点的年龄,并不是没有用的:是啊,这片别人所轻视的田地却是有收成的;是啊,这片田地是宜于播种的。努力啊,当你的气力和你的青春还可以应付的时候,不久那使你

Besides, they've more knowledge of the thing, and have that practice that alone makes the artist. With elegance they repair the marks of time, and take good care that they don't appear old. As you wish, they'll perform in a thousand positions: no painting's ever contrived to show more ways. They don't have to be aroused to pleasure: man and woman equally deliver what delights. I hate sex that doesn't provide release for both: that's why the touch of boys is less desirable. I hate a girl who gives because she has to, and, arid herself, thinks only of her spinning. Pleasure's no joy to me that's given out of duty: let no girl be dutiful to me. I like to hear a voice confessing to her rapture, which begs me to hold back, and keep on going. I gaze at the dazed eyes of my frantic mistress: she's exhausted, and won't let herself be touched for ages. Nature doesn't give those joys to raw youths, that often come so easily beyond thirty-five. The hasty drink the new and unfermented: pour a vintage wine for me, matured in the cask, from an ancient consulship. Not till it's grown can

佝偻的衰年就要悄悄地来临了。用你的桨劈开海水,或是用你的犁分开泥土,或是用你习武有力的手拿着杀人的武器,或是用你男子的精力和殷勤去供奉妇人。这最后的一种就像是在军队服役;这最后的一种也能够得到利益。再者这些妇人对于爱情的工作都是十分渊博的,而且她们都是很有经验的,因为只有经验才能造就艺术家。她们用化妆遮盖了时间的损害,又小心翼翼地不露出老妇人的样子来,她会体贴你的心情,做出许多姿态来,随便哪一集春画都没有她的变化多。在她的身上,幽欢不是由人工的激动生出来的;那真正温柔的幽欢应当是男子和女子都有份的。我恨那些不是两方同样热烈的拥抱(这就是我觉得少女兴味很少的缘故),我恨那些"应该"委身过来而委身过来的女子,她一点儿也感觉不到什么,还在想着她的纺锤。那种因为是本分而允许我的欢乐在我看来是不能成为欢乐的,我不要一个女子对我有什么本分。我愿意听见她泄露出她所感受到欢乐的声音,和恳求我缓缓地来以延长她的幸福的声音。我爱看她沉醉在逸乐中,懒洋洋地凝视着我,或是为爱情而憔悴,长

the plane tree bear the sun, and naked feet destroy a new-laid lawn. I suppose you'd prefer Hermione to Helen, and was Medusa any better than her mother? Then, he who wants to come to his love late, earns a valuable prize, if he'll only wait.

阿波罗

久地不愿别人去碰她一下。可是这种利益，老天是不会赐予青年人的：要到中年才能够遇到。性急的人去喝新酒吧，我呢，你倒一杯盛在一个双持中的我们祖先在执政官时代酿的陈酒给我喝吧！槲树要经过许多岁月才能够抵抗斐菩斯[249]的光，而那新割过的草地却伤了我们的脚。什么！在海尔迷奥奈[250]和海伦之间你宁愿要海尔迷奥奈吗？而高尔葛[251]又胜过她的母亲吗？总之你要品尝成熟的爱情果子，只要你不固执，你总会如愿以偿的。

ⅩⅨ: Don't Rush

See, the knowing bed receives two lovers: halt, Muse, at the closed doors of the room. Flowing words will be said, by themselves, without you: and that left hand won't lie idle on the bed. Fingers will find what will arouse those parts, where love's dart is dipped in secrecy. Hector did it once with vigour, for Andromache, and wasn't only useful in the wars. And great Achilles did it for his captive maid, when he lay in his sweet bed, weary from the fight. You let yourself be touched by hands, Briseis, that were still dyed with Trojan blood. And was that what overjoyed you, lascivious girl, those conquering fingers approaching your body? Trust me, love's pleasure's not to be hurried, but to be felt enticingly with lingering delays. When you've reached the place, where a girl loves to be touched, don't let modesty prevent you touching her. You'll see her eyes flickering

19.不要匆忙

现在那床已经接受了我们一对有情人:缪赛啊,在他们卧室紧闭的门前止步吧! 没有你,他们也许会找出许多话来的,而且在床上他们的手是不会有空闲的。他们的手指也会在阿谟尔喜欢把他的箭射过去的神秘地方找些事情来做。从前那最英武的海克笃尔就是这样地对付盎特罗玛黑的,海克笃尔所擅长的并不只是打仗。那伟大的阿岂赖斯也是如此对付他的利尔奈索斯女俘虏[252]的,当他战乏了睡在一张柔软的床上,勃丽赛伊丝啊,你一点也不畏惧受到那双经常染着特洛伊人血的手的抚爱。陶醉的美人啊,那时你所最爱的,不就是那胜利者的手紧搂着你的那种感觉吗?相信我,不要太急于达到陶醉的境地;你必须要经过许多次延迟,不知不觉地达到那种境地。当你已经找到一个女子最喜欢受爱抚的地方,你必须不怕羞地去爱抚。于是你就会看见你的情妇的眼睛里闪着一道颤动的光,像

with tremulous brightness, as sunlight often flashes from running water. Moans and loving murmurs will arise, and sweet sighs, and playful and fitting words. But don't desert your mistress by cramming on more sail, or let her overtake you in your race; hasten to the goal together: that's the fullness of pleasure, when man and woman lie there equally spent. This is the pace you should indulge in, when you're given time for leisure, and fear does not urge on the secret work. When delay's not safe, lean usefully on the oar, and plunge your spur into the galloping horse.

文艺女神缪赛

水波所反映出来的太阳光一样。随后是一阵夹着甜蜜的低语声和怨语声的醉人呻吟，和那兴奋的爱情蜜语。可是你不要把帆张得太满，把你的情妇落在后面，也不要让她走在你的前面。目的就是要同时到达。当男子和女子两个都同时战败了，一点气力也没有地瘫在那里，那正是无上的欢乐啊！当你悠闲自在的时候和没有恐怖来催你匆匆了事的时候，这就是你应该遵照的规则，可是当延迟会发生危险的时候，你应当屈身在桨上竭力地划着，而且用刺马轮刺你的骏马。

XX: The Task's Complete, But Now...

The end of the work's at hand: grateful youth grant me the palm, and set the wreathe of myrtle on my perfumed hair. As Podalirius with his art of medicine, among the Greeks, was great, Achilles with his right hand, Nestor his wisdom, Calchas great as a prophet, Ajax in arms, Automedon

艾阿古斯的孙子

20.任务完成,但还……

我的大著快要结束了。满怀感恩的青年人啊,给我棕榈,请在我薰香的头发上给我戴一顶桁榴花冠[253]。就像包达里虑思[254]在希腊人中以医术出名,艾阿古斯的孙子[255]以勇敢出名,奈思多尔[256]以机警出名,就像迦尔卡思[257]因为占卜,戴拉蒙的儿子[258]因为统兵,沃岛美东[259]因为驾车,我

as a charioteer，so am I in love. Celebrate me as a poet，men，speak my praises，let my name be sung throughout the world. I've given you weapons：Vulcan gave Achilles his：excel with the gifts you're given，as he excelled. But whoever overcomes an Amazon with my sword，write on the spoils "Ovid was my master."

Behold，you tender girls ask for rules for yourselves：well yours then will be the next task for my pen!

戴拉蒙的儿子

呢，我的出名在于我精于爱术。多情的男子，歌颂你们的诗人啊，让我的姓氏为全世界所歌唱。我把武器提供给你们；胡尔迦怒思把武器提供给阿岂赖斯[260]，愿我的礼品能够带给你们胜利，就像阿岂赖斯获得胜利一样。而且我希望凡是用我所赠的剑的人们在战胜一个阿马逊人[261]之后，在他们的战利品上这样写："奥维德是我的老师。"

可是现在那些多情的少女们前来向我求教了。年轻的美人儿，为了你们，我才遗下后面的诗篇。

第三卷　女人的资本

Book Ⅲ　Woman friend

I: It's Time to Teach You Girls

I've given the Greeks arms, against Amazons: arms remain, to give to you Penthesilea, and your Amazon troop. Go equal to the fight: let them win, those who are favoured by Venus, and her Boy, who flies through all the world. It's not fair for armed men to battle with naked girls: that would be shameful, men, even if you win.

班黛西莱阿

1.女性教育的时间

我武装希腊人与阿马逊人战斗，班黛西莱阿[262]啊，现在我要拿起武器给你和你骁勇的军队了，用相同的武器去上阵啊，胜利属于那第奥奈[263]和张着翅膀飞行在全宇宙的孩子[264]所宠幸的人。让你们毫无防御地遭受武装得很好的敌人的攻击是不应该的。而你呢，男子，这样即使战胜了也是可羞的。

Someone will say: "Why add venom to the snake, and betray the sheepfold to the rabid she-wolf?" Beware of loading the crime of the many onto the few: let the merits of each separate girl be seen. Though Menelaus has Helen, and Agamemnon has Clytemnestra, her sister, to charge with crime, though Amphiaraus, and his horses too, came living to the Styx, through the wickedness of Eriphyle, Penelope was faithful to her husband for all ten years of his waging war, and his ten years wandering. Think of Protesilaus, and Laodamia who they say followed her marriage partner, died before her time. Alcestis, his wife, redeemed Admetus's life with her

巴加沙的女子

可能有人要说了:"你为什么还要拿新的毒液给蝮蛇啊?你为什么要把羊圈打开让凶猛的雌狼进来啊? "请你们不要把几个女人的罪加到一切女子的身上去,我们应当从她们各人的行为来进行判断。阿特拉思的幼子和长子[265]可以提出一个严重的责备,一个是对于海伦的,一个是对于海伦的姊姊[266]的;达拉奥思[267]的女儿爱丽菲拉[268]的罪,是活活地将骑着马的奥伊克葛思的儿子[269]赶到司底克思河岸上[270]去,但是珮耐洛珀却在她丈夫十年征战十年漂泊的时间里坚守着贞节。请想想费拉古思的孙子[271]和那在如花的年纪就追随他到黄泉去的人[272]吧! 巴加沙的女子[273]

own: the wife, for the man, was borne to the husband's funeral. "Capaneus, receive me! Let us mingle our ashes." Evadne cried, and leapt into the flames.

Virtue herself is named and worshipped as a woman too: it's no wonder that she delights her followers. Yet their aims are not required for my art, smaller sails are suited to my boat, Only playful passions will be learnt from me: I'll teach girls the ways of being loved. Women don't brandish flames or cruel bows: I rarely see men harmed by their weapons.

云海尔古赖斯

用自己的生命把他的丈夫——费莱思的儿子[274]——的生命重新买回来了。"接受我呀,加巴纳思[275],我们的骨灰至少要合在一起的。"伊菲阿丝[276]说着,便纵身跳到了焚尸场中。

德行是以女子为衣以女子为名的,她受到它的恩宠难道有什么值得奇怪的吗?然而我的艺术却不是教育这些伟大灵魂的,我的船只要较小一点的帆就够了。我只教授轻飘的爱情。我将教女人如何才能惹人怜爱。女人不懂得抵抗阿谟尔的火和利箭,我觉得他的箭穿入女子的心比穿入

Men often cheat: it's seldom tender girls, and, if you check, they're rarely accused of fraud. Falsely, Jason left Medea, already a mother: he took another bride to himself. As far as you knew, Theseus, the sea birds fed on Ariadne, left all by herself on an unknown island! Ask why one road's called Nine-Times and hear how the woods, weeping, shed their leaves for Phyllis. Though he might be famed for piety, Aeneas, your guest, supplied the sword, Dido, and the reason for your death. What destroyed you all, I ask? Not knowing how to love: your art was lacking; love lasts long through art. You still might lack it now; but, before my eyes, stood Venus herself, and ordered me to teach you. She said to me, then: "What have the poor girls done, an unarmed crowd betrayed to well-armed men? Two books of their tricks have been composed: let this lot too be instructed by your warnings. Stesichorus who spoke against Helen's unchastity, soon sang her praises in a happier key. If I know you well (don't harm the cultured girls now!) this favour will always be asked of you while

男子的心更深。男子们总是在欺人的;纤弱的女人们欺人的却不多,你先把女性研究一下吧,你就会发现负心的很少。那已经做了母亲生在法西斯岸上的女子[277],被约松欺骗和抛弃;艾松的儿子[278]还在怀间接受了另外一个新娘[279]。戴设斯啊,阿丽亚特娜独自被弃在她所不认识的地方,差一点就做了海鸟的食料[280]。你去考查一下为什么有一条路叫做"九条路",答案是:树林哭泣着菲丽丝[281],把它们的叶子落在她的坟上。你的宾客拥有虔诚信徒的名誉,然而,艾丽莎[282]啊,你却从他那里接受到了一把利剑和失望,你就自杀了。不幸的人们啊,我将告诉你们悲惨遭遇的原因:你们不懂得恋爱。你们缺少艺术,而使爱情持久的就是艺术。即使是在今天她们仍旧不懂得,可是那岂带拉的女神[283]命我把我的课程教授给女子。她现身在我的面前对我说:"那些不幸的女子有什么地方得罪你了吗?你将她们那些没有抵抗力的队伍投到武装得很好的男子们那儿去。那些男子,你已经为他们著了两卷书,让他们精通了爱术,女性自然也应当轮到学习你的功课了。起初贬骂生在代拉泊奈[284]的妻子的人随后在一

you live." She spoke, and she gave me a leaf, and a few myrtle berries (since her hair was crowned with myrtle): I felt received power too; purer airglowed, and a whole weight lifted from my spirit. While wit works, seek your orders here girls, those that modesty, principles and your rules allow. Be mindful first that old age will come to you: so don't be timid and waste any of your time. Have fun while it's allowed, while your years are in their prime: the years go by like flowing waters: The wave that's past can't be

阿丽亚特娜

篇更幸福的诗中歌颂她了[285]。假如我很熟悉曾经爱过女人的你，请你不要让她们吃亏吧！这个服务的报偿，是你在一生之中都可以要求的。"当她站在我前面的时候这样说着，又从她头上戴的石榴冠上，摘下了一片叶子和几粒石榴给我。当我接受的时候，我感到了一个神明的感应：空气是格外光辉而清净的，而工作的疲倦又是绝对不会压在我心上的。当维纳斯感兴趣的时候，女子啊，到这儿来求学吧，贞节和法律都准许你，你的利益也在邀请你。从今以后请你想一想那不久就要来到的衰老吧，这样你便不会把时光虚掷了。当你还能玩的时候，当你还在生命的春日里时，娱乐啊！年华像水一样地流逝了，逝波是永远不会回到水的源头的，

recalled again, the hour that's past never can return. Life's to be used: life slips by on swift feet, what was good at first, nothing as good will follow. Those stalks that wither I saw as violets: from that thorn-bush to me a dear garland was given. There'll be a time when you, who now shut out your lover, will lie alone, and aged, in the cold of night, nor find your entrance damaged by some nocturnal quarrel, nor your threshold sprinkled with roses at dawn. How quickly (ah me!) the sagging flesh wrinkles, and the colour, there, is lost from the bright cheek. And hairs that you'll swear were grey from your girlhood will spring up all over your head overnight. Snakes shed their old age with their fragile skin, antlers that are cast make the stag seem young: un-aided our beauties flee: pluck the flower, which, if not plucked, will of itself, shamefully, fall. Add that the time of youth is shortened by childbirth: the field's exhausted by continual harvest. Endymion causes you no blushes, on Latmos, Moon, nor is Cephalus the rosy goddess of Dawn's shameful prize. Though Adonis

时间一旦过去了就同样地去而不返了。不要辜负了大好的时光,它如此快地飞逝了!今天总是不如昨天好的。在这些荆棘丛生的地方,我曾经看见紫罗兰漫山开遍,我曾经用这枝长满刺的荆棘编织了一个很好的花冠。你现在年纪还轻,推开你的情郎,可是当有一个时刻到来,衰老又孤单,你夜间将在孤冷的床上颤栗着。你的门不会被情敌们夜间的争执所打破,而且在早晨,你也不可能看见门槛上铺满了蔷薇。啊,我们的皮肤那样快就起皱了!我们灿烂的容颜那样快就改变了!你发誓说你做少女的时候就有的白发不久就要爬满头了。蛇脱了皮也就脱去了它的衰老,鹿换了角也就又变得年轻了;可是时间从我们那里夺去的长处是什么都无法补救的:花开堪折直须折,莫待无花空折枝啊!多生孩子能够使人老得快一些,收获的次数太多,田地也会枯竭的。“月”啊,安第米雍[286]在拉特摩司山[287]上没有使你害羞,而凯发路思[288]被蔷薇手指的女神[289]抢得也没有什么可羞愧的,而阿陶尼斯是更不用说了,维纳斯到现在还在为他哭泣,她的儿子艾耐阿斯和哈尔穆宜阿[290]是从哪里来的呢?平凡的女子

was given to Venus, whom she mourns to this day, where did she get Aeneas, and Harmonia, from? O mortal girls go to the goddesses for your examples, and don't deny your delights to loving men. Even if you're deceived, what do you lose? It's all intact: though a thousand use it, nothing's destroyed that way. Iron crumbles, stone's worn away with use: that part's sufficient, and escapes all fear of harm. Who objects to taking light from a light nearby? Who hoards the vast waters of the hollow deep? So why should any woman say: "Not now"? Tell me, why waste the water if you're not going to use it? Nor does my voice say sell it, just don't be afraid of casual loss: your gifts are freed from loss. But I'm blown about by greater gusts of wind, while we're in harbour, may you ride the gentle breeze.

啊，你们要以神仙为榜样，不要拒绝你们情郎所希望的，你们可以给他们的那些欢乐。假设他们欺骗了你们，你们会损失些什么呢？你们所有的一切，你们仍旧保留着。一千个人可以得到你们的恩宠，可是他们不能损失你的万一。时间久了，铁石都会被磨穿，可是我所说的那件东西却能够抵抗一切，你也不会有丝毫的损失。一支蜡烛在点燃另一支蜡烛的时候会失去光亮吗？小小的一勺海水会让沧海枯竭吗？可是曾经有一个女子回答男子说：“没有办法。”什么？你会损失什么呢？不过是你拿来洗浴的水吧！我并不是劝你委身于一切过路的人，不过请求你不要怀疑会有什么损失吧：在你赐予的时候，你是没有任何损失的。不久我就要一阵更有力的风，现在我还在港口，一阵轻风已经足够帮助我前进了！

Ⅱ: Take Care with How You Look

I'll start with how you look: good wine comes from vines that are looked after, tall crops stand in cultivated soil. Beauty's a gift of the gods: how many can boast it? The larger number among you lack such gifts. Taking pains brings beauty: beauty neglected dies, even though it's like that of Venus, the Idalian goddess. If girls of old didn't cultivate their bodies in that way, well they had no cultivated men in those days; if Andromache was dressed in healthy clothes, what wonder? Her husband was a rough soldier? Do you suppose Ajax's wife would come to him all smart, when his outer layer was seven hides of an ox? There was crude simplicity before: now Rome is golden, and owns the vast wealth of the conquered world. Look what the Capitol is

2.注重外貌与装束

我先从冶容术开始;栽培得好好的葡萄能够酿出很多的酒,耕耘得好好的田地收获也就丰富。美貌是天赐的礼物,可是能以美貌来骄傲的又有几个!你们之中有许多人都没有接受到这种赐予。冶容术会给你们一张俊俏的脸蛋儿,一张脸儿如果不事修饰,那么即使它像伊达良女神[291]的脸儿一样,也会失去它的一切光彩。假如从前的女子们不关心冶容,那么她们的丈夫也就不会关心她们了。假如那披在盎特罗玛黑身上的衫子是用精布制作的,有什么值得诧异吗?她的丈夫[292]不过是一个粗鲁的士兵。有人可曾看见阿约思的妻子装束华美地去见她的以七张牛皮做盾的丈夫吗?过去是一种乡村的淳朴统治着,现在的罗马则是被璀璨的黄金装饰,并且还拥有它所征服的全世界的浩漫财富。你可以看看现在的加比都良[293]和过去的加比都良,人们会说现在供奉的是另外一个裘比德。元

now, and what it was: you'd say it belonged to a different Jove. The Senate-House, now worthy of such debates, was made of wattle when Tatius held the kingship. Where the Palatine now gleams with Apollo and our leaders, what was that but pasture for ploughmen's oxen? Others may delight in ancient times; I congratulate myself on having been born just now: this age suits my nature. Not because stubborn gold's mined now from the earth, or choice shells come to us from farthest shores: nor

裘比德神

老院现在很适合那庄严的集会，在达丢思王[294]治国的时候，它不过是一所简单的茅舍而已。巴拉丁山，在那里有阿普罗和我们的领袖们保护的灿烂大厦[295]，在那时是什么呢？只是一片放养耕牛的牧场而已。让别人去夸耀往昔吧，我呢，我是非常庆幸生在今天这个时代的。现在的这个世纪是合乎我的脾胃的。这不是因为在今天人们从地下采取了黄金，或是人们从各处海岸拾取珠贝；也不是因为人们采掘大理石而使山消减了下去，或是我们的大坝把绿色的波涛打退了。而是因为现在人们讲究

because mountains shrink as marble's quarried, or because blue waters retreat from the piers: but because civilisation's here, and no crudity remains, in our age, that survives from our ancient ancestors. You too shouldn't weight your ears with costly stones, that dusky India gathers in its green waters, nor show yourself in stiff clothes sewn with gold, wealth which you court us with, often makes us flee.

达丢思王

冶容之术，而长久留存在我们祖先那个时代的鄙野，到我们的这个时候已经不存在了。可你们也不要把那些黑色的印度人在绿水里采来的高价宝石挂在耳朵上，也不要披着那妨碍你们轻盈的、坠着黄金的锦衣。这种场面，你们本来是想用来引诱我们的，结果却反而把我们吓跑了。

Ⅲ: Taste and Elegance in Hair and Dress

We're captivated by elegance: don't ignore your hair: beauty's granted or denied by a hand's touch. There isn't only one style: choose what suits each one, and consult your mirror in advance. An oval-shaped head suggests a plain parting: that's how Laodamia arranged her hair. A round face asks for a small knot on the top, leaving the forehead free, showing the ears. One girl should throw her hair over both shoulders: like Phoebus when he takes up the lyre to sing. Another tied up behind, in Diana's usual style, when, skirts tucked up, she seeks the frightened quarry. Blown tresses suit this girl, loosely scattered: that one's encircled by tight-bound hair. This one delights in being adorned by tortoiseshell from Cyllene: that one presents a likeness to the curves of a wave. But you'll no more number the acorns on oak branches, or bees on Hybla,

3.品味高雅的发型与服饰

素雅的装束才会使你惹人怜爱。不要把你们的头发弄乱。梳头妈妈的手能够增加美丽或是减损美丽。梳头有许许多多的式样,每人选择一个适合自己的式样,第一重要的就是要照一照镜子。脸形长的需要将头发分梳在额头上,不需要什么装饰,这就是拉奥达米阿的梳法。把头发梳起来,在额前梳成一个小髻,让耳朵露出来,这种梳法最适宜圆脸的女子。有的少妇让长发披拂在肩头,和谐的斐菩斯啊,正像你一样,当你在调琴的时候。有的却应该梳起辫子,像那老是穿着短短的衫子在林中追逐猛兽的第阿娜一样。有的飘着卷曲的头发使我们着迷,有的把头发梳得平平的,贴在鬓边,使我们销魂。有的应该簪着玳瑁的梳子做装饰,有的应该把她的头发卷起像波纹。浓密橡树的橡实,希勃拉山[296]的蜜蜂,阿尔卑斯山[297]的野兽都可以计算,而每天出来的梳头新花样却是数也数不

wild beasts on Alpine mountains, than I can possibly count so many fashions: every new day adds another new style. And tangled hair suits many girls; often you'd think it's been hanging loose since yesterday; it's just combed. Art imitates chance: when Hercules, in captured Oechalia, saw Iole like that, he said: "I love that girl." So you Bacchus, lifted forsaken Ariadne, into your chariot, while the Satyrs gave their cries. Oh how kind nature is to your beauty, how many ways you have to repair the damage! We're sadly exposed, and our hair, snatched at by time, falls

阿达马思

清。随便的梳妆对于许多人是相配的，这种梳妆别人以为是前一日梳了现在又重新整理一下的。艺术是应该模仿偶然的。在攻破城池之后，伊奥莱[298]现身于海尔古赖斯之前也是这个模样，海尔古赖斯一见到她就说："我所爱的就是这个人。"而你，被抛弃的格诺梭思地方的女儿[299]，当你在刹帝鲁斯们的"曷荷艾"呼声中被巴古斯举到他车上的时候，你也是这个模样的。女子啊，老天对于你们的娇媚可爱是多么愿意出力帮忙啊，你们有千种的方法来补救时间的损害！至于我们男子们呢，我们简直就没有

like the leaves stripped by the north wind. A woman dyes the grey with German herbs, and seeks a better colour by their art: a woman shows herself in dense bought curls, instead of her own, pays cash for another's. No blushes shown: you can see them coming, openly, before the eyes of Hercules and the Virgin Muses Choir.

What to say about dress? Don't ask for brocade, or wools dyed purple with Tyrian murex. With so many cheaper colours having appeared, it's crazy to bear your fortune on your back! See, the sky's colour, when the sky's without a cloud, no warm south-westerly threatening heavy rain. See, what to you, you'll say, looks similar to that fleece, on which Phrixus and Helle once escaped fierce Ino: this resembles the waves, and also takes its name from the waves. I might have thought the sea-nymphs clothed with this veil. That's like saffron-flowers: dressed in saffron robes, the dew-wet goddess yokes her shining horses; this, Paphian myrtle: this, purple amethyst, dawn roses, and the Thracian crane's grey.

办法去掩饰时间的损害，我们被岁月所带去的头发，就像被北风吹落的树叶一样凋落。女人呢，用格尔马奈[300]的草汁来染她们的白发；这种技术给予她们一种假借的颜色，比天然的颜色更好看。女人呢，装着她刚买来的茸厚的头发走过来，而且，只要花几个钱，别人的头发就改变了她们。而且她们即使是在海尔古赖斯和缪赛们面前买假发也不会感到害羞的[301]。

关于衣饰我该说些什么呢？那种使用华丽的镶边并且用帝路司红染过的毛织物和我有什么关系呢？价格便宜些的颜色多着呢！为什么要把你全部的财产全都背在身上呢？你看这天蓝，就像是被南风吹散了雨云的蓝天一样，你看这黄金，这正是从伊诺[302]的毒汁中救出弗里若克思和海莱[303]的公羊的颜色。这绿色是模仿海水的，由海水而得到它的名字[304]。我很愿意相信这是水上仙子的衣衫。这个颜色就像郁金草，就是那沾着露水驾着光芒骏马的女神[305]的郁金草衣衫的颜色，在那里你可以找到巴福斯番石榴的颜色，这里有紫红宝石色，苍白的蔷薇色或者是脱拉岂阿

Your chestnuts are not lacking, Amaryllis, and almonds: and wax gives its name to various wools. As many as the flowers the new world, in warm spring, bears when vine-buds wake, and dark winter vanishes, as many or more dyes the wool drinks; choose, decisively; since all are not suitable for everyone. Dark-grey suits snow-white skin; dark-grey suited Briseis; when she was carried off, then she also wore dark-grey. White suits the dark: you looked pleasing, Andromeda, in white; so dressed, the island of Seriphos was ruled by you.

爱美是女人的天性

鹤羽毛的颜色。我们还有,阿马里力思[306]啊,你所爱吃的栗子的颜色,杏仁的颜色;和因蜜蜡而得名的布的颜色。毛织物所染的颜色,就和春天的温暖使葡萄抽芽又驱逐了那闲懒的冬天时地上所出现的花朵的颜色一样多,而且也许还要更多些。在这许多颜色之间,你留意选择吧!因为一切颜色并不都适合一切的女子。黑色最适合皮肤皎白的女子;黑色是适合勃丽赛伊丝的,当她被掠走的时候,她正穿着黑色的衣裳。白色最适合棕色皮肤的女子:凯弗斯的女儿[307],一件白色的衣服使你变得格外娇媚,这就是你降落到塞里福司岛[308]时所穿的衣服颜色。

Ⅳ:Make-Up，but in Private

But in private how near I was to warning you，no rankness of the wild goatunder your armpits，no legs bristling with harsh hair! But I'm not teaching girls from the Caucasian hills，or those who drink your waters，Mysian Caicus. So why remind you not to let your teeth get blackened，be being lazy，and to wash your face each morning in water? You know how to acquire whiteness with a layer of powder: she who doesn't blush by blood，indeed，blushes by art. You make good the naked edges of your eyebrows，and hide your natural cheeks with little patches. It's no shame to highlight your eyes with thinned ashes，or saffron grown by your banks，bright Cydnus. It's I who spoke of facial treatments for your beauty，a little book，but one whose labour took great care. There too you can find protection against faded looks: my art's no idle thing in your behalf.

4.隐蔽地化妆

我正要告诉你不要让你的腋下有狐臭，不要让你的腿上矗起粗毛。可是我的功课并不是教授那些住在高加赛山岩下的女子和喝着米西阿加伊古司河水的女子的。你们不要疏忽，一定要把牙齿弄干净，不然每天早晨在梳妆台上洗净了脸又有什么用呢?你们会用铅粉来涂白你们的脸儿，皮肤天生不娇红的人可以用人工使它变红。你们的艺术还能够补救眉毛离得太开的毛病，还能用"颜妆"来遮住你们年龄的痕迹。你们更不要因为用细灰或是生在澄清的启特诺斯河岸上的郁金草涂在眼圈上来增加你们眼睛的光彩而感到害羞。关于那些能够使你们美丽的方法，我已经著有专论[309]，虽然都是短短的，却很精细重要。不被老天所宠幸的年轻女子，你们也可以到那儿去讨救兵，我的艺术是不吝以有益的话来教导你们的。

Still, don't let your lover find cosmetic bottleson your dressing table: art delights in its hidden face. Who's not offended by cream smeared all over your face, when it runs in fallen drops to your warm breast? Don't those ointments smell? Even if they are sent from Athens, they're oils extracted from the unwashed fleece of a sheep. Don't apply preparations of deer marrow openly, and I don't approve of openly cleaning your teeth: it makes for beauty, but it's not beautiful to watch; many things that please when done, are ugly in the doing; What now carries the signature of busy Myron was once dumb mass, hard stone; to make a ring, first crush the golden ore; the dress you wear, was greasy wool. That was rough marble, now it forms a famous statue, naked Venus squeezing water from her wet

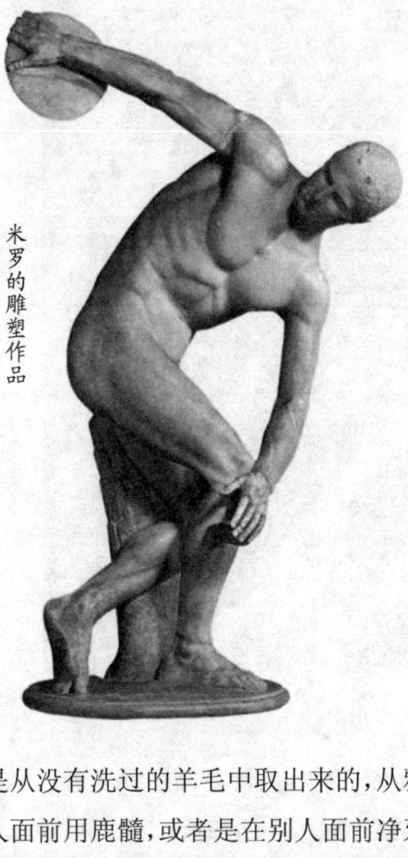
米罗的雕塑作品

可是不要使你的情郎瞥见你坐在摊满了小盒子的桌边：要让艺术使你美丽而又不被别人看见。看见那酒滓儿涂满你们的脸，因为重而坠下来流到你的胸前，谁会不厌恶呢？用脂质液做原料的粉的气味是怎样的一种气味啊！虽然这种液体是从没有洗过的羊毛中取出来的，从雅典运来的。我劝你最好不要在别人面前用鹿髓，或者是在别人面前净牙齿。我知道这些能够使你格外娇媚，但是那种光景却是很不体面的，多少东西在做的时候是何等的难看，而当做好之后却能够使我们感到愉悦！今天你们看看这些雕像，勤劳的米罗[310]的杰作，在从前不过只是一块顽石，一块不成形的金属。要做一个金戒指是先要捶金的，你现在所穿的衣服过去只是一些不干净的羊毛。

hair. We'll think you too are sleeping while you do your face: fit to be seen after the final touches. Why should I know the source of the brightness in your looks? Close your bedroom door! Why betray unfinished work? There are many things it's right men shouldn't know: most things offend if you don't keep them secret. The golden figures shining from the ornate theatre, examine them, you'll despise them: gilding hiding wood; but the crowd's not allowed to approach them till they're done, and till your beauty's ready banish men. But I don't forbid your hair being freely

裸体的维纳斯

这大理石像,从前只是一块不成东西的石头,而现在却已经成为著名的雕像,这是绞去头发上水的裸体维纳斯[31]。同样,当你们为自己的美下功夫的时候,你们让我们以为你们还在睡着吧。等你们梳洗完毕之后走出来,好处就多了。为什么要让我知道你们脸儿皎白的原因呢?把你们卧室的门关起来吧!为什么要把那不完全的工程显露出来呢?有许许多多事情男子们是应当懵懂的,如果内幕被我们看穿了,差不多不管什么外表

combed, so that it falls, loosely spread, across your shoulders. Beware especially lest you're irritable then, or are always loosening your failed hairstyle again. Leave your maid alone: I hate those who scratch her face with their nails, or prick the arm they've snatched at with a pin. She'll curse her mistress's head at every touch, as she weeps, bleeding, on the hateful tresses. If you're hair's appalling, set a guard at your threshold, or always have it done at Bona Dea's fertile temple. I was once suddenly announced arriving at some girl's: in her confusion she put her hair on wrong way round. May such cause of cruel shame come to my enemies, and that disgrace be reserved for Parthian girls. Hornless cows are ugly, fields are ugly without grass, and bushes without leaves, and a head without its hair.

我们都会厌恶的。剧场上金色的饰物,你仔细去看看:那不过是在一块木头上包了一层薄薄的金!戏没有演完是不准看客走近去看的,因此你们应当在男子不在旁边的时候化妆,这是同样的理由。然而我却并不禁止你们在我们面前梳理头发,我爱看你们的发丝披拂在你们的肩头。可是你应当不会让人几次三番地拆了又梳,梳了又拆。不要让你们的梳头妈妈对你们有所恐惧,我恨那些用指甲抓破梳头妈妈的脸和用发针刺她手臂的女人们。她诅咒她女主人的头,那个她还捧在手上的头,同时,她流着血把她的眼泪滴到那可恶的头发上。一切不能夸耀自己头发的女子应该在门边放一个岗哨,或者是到善良女神[312]的庙里去梳头。有一天,他们向一位女子通报我突然光临,在匆忙之中,她把假发都装倒了。希望这样大的侮辱,都加到我们仇敌的身上去吧!愿这种耻辱留给巴尔底[313]的女子吧!一只牛没有角、一片地没有草、一株树没有叶和一个头没有头发都是极其丑陋的。

Ⅴ:Conceal Your Defects

I've not come to teach Semele or Leda, or Sidon's Europa, carried through the waves by that deceptive bull, or Helen, whom Menelaus, being no fool, reclaimed, and you, Paris, her Trojan captor, also no fool, withheld. The crowd come to be taught, girls pretty and plain: and always the greater part are not-so-good. The beautiful ones don't seek art and instruction: they have their dowry, beauty potent without art; the sailor rests secure when the sea's calm; when it's swollen, he uses every aid. Still, faultless forms are rare: conceal your faults, and hide your body's defects as best you may. If you're short sit down, lest, standing, you

赛美莱

5.掩饰缺点

赛美莱[314]或者莱黛[315]啊,我的课程并不是教你们的,被一头假牛载到海外的西同女子[316]啊,我的课程也不是教你的,更不是教海伦的。这海伦,美奈拉乌思啊,你索取她是理所应当的,而你,抢她的特洛伊人啊,你不放她也是有理由的。我的众多女弟子中美的丑的都有,而丑的更是占据了大多数!美的女子不一定需要我的功课的帮助和教导,她们有属于她们自己的美,并不需要艺术来施展它的权威。当大海平静的时候,舵工可以平安地休息,当起了风浪的时候,他便离不开他的舵了。可是没有缺点的脸儿是很少见的!隐藏了这些缺点,而且,尽量减少你身上的不完善。假如你身材矮小,你就坐着,因为即使你站着的时候也会让人误以为

seem to sit; and commit your smallness to your couch: there also, so your measure can't be taken, let a shawl drop over your feet to hide them. If you're very slender, wear a full dress, and walk aboutin clothes that hang loosely from your shoulders. A pale girl scatters bright stripes across her body, the darker then have recourse to linen from Alexandria. Let an ugly foot be hidden in snow-white leather; and don't loose the bands from skinny legs. Thin padding suits those with high shoulder blades: a good brassiere goes with a meagre chest.

斯巴达王登达勒思的妻子莱黛

你是坐着的；假如你是一个矮子，你就应当躺在床上，这样躺着，别人也就看不出你的身材了，还要用一件衫子把你的脚遮住。如果身材太瘦小，你就要穿厚布的衣服，再用一件很大的氅披在你的肩上。惨白的脸还要搽上胭脂，棕色的脸则要向法鲁斯的鱼[317]讨救兵。畸形的脚需要藏在精细的白皮鞋里，干瘦的腿千万不要不裹皮带就露出来让别人看见。薄薄的小垫子补救了肩头的高低不齐，假如胸脯是扁平的，就要遮一块胸袜。

Ⅵ:Be Modest in Laughter and Movement

If your fingers are stumpy and your nails unsightly, don't gesticulate when you are talking. If your breath is strong, you should never talk when your stomach's empty, and always keep some distance away from your lover. If you're teeth are blackened, large, or not in line from birth, laughing would be a fatal error.

Who'd believe it? Girls must even learn to laugh, they seek to acquire beauty also in this way. Laugh modestly, a small dimple either

翁伯利人

6.端庄的微笑和举止

假如你的手指太粗或者你的指甲太粗糙,说话的时候千万不要做手势。口气太重的女子,在肚子饿的时候千万不要说话,而且对男子说话的时候,也应当站得远远的。假如你的牙齿太黑、太长、太不整齐,那么你一笑就大糟特糟了。

谁会相信呢?女子甚至还要学习如何笑,这艺术能够使她们格外的娇媚可爱。嘴不要张得太大,要使你的颊上起两个小小的酒窝儿,使下唇

side, the teeth mostly concealed by the lips. Don't strain your lungs with continual laughter, but let something soft and feminine ring out. One girl will distort her face perversely by guffawing; another shakes with laughter, you'd think she's crying. That one laughs stridently in a hateful manner, like a mangy ass braying at the shameful mill. Where does art not penetrate? They're taught to cry, with propriety, they weep when and how they wish. Why! Aren't true words cheated by the voice, and tongues forced to make lisping sounds to order? Charm's in a defect: they try to speak badly; they're taught, when they can speak, to speak less. Weigh all this with care, since it's for you: learn to carry yourself in a feminine way. And not the least part of charm is in walking: it attracts men you

娇媚可爱的女子

盖住上面的牙尖。笑的时候不要太长久，笑的次数也不要太多，这样你的笑就温柔、细腻，人人爱看了。有些女子扭曲了她们的嘴大笑，做出很难看的样子；有的女子大声地笑着，我们听起来却像是在哭。还有一些女子用粗蠢而又不怎么悦耳的声音来扰乱我们的耳朵，正像那拉磨老母驴的叫声一样。艺术哪里伸展不到啊？女子甚至还应该学习如何才能哭得好看呢，她们流着眼泪，在她们要哭和好像要哭的时候。那些吃了重要的字母和勉强使她的舌头格格不吐的女人我又该怎么说呢？这种读音的毛病在她们是一种娇媚可爱，她们应该学习如何才能说得更不好些。这是琐细的事，可是既然是有用的，那么你就得细心研究。你们还要学习适合女子的步法。在步履中有一种不可忽视的美，它能够吸引或是推开一个你们所

don't know, or sends them running. One moves her hips with art, catches the breeze with flowing robes, and points her toes daintily; another walks like the wife of a red-faced Umbrian, feet wide apart, and with huge paces. But there's measure here as in most things: both the rustic's stride, and the more affected step should be foregone. Still, let the parts of your lower shoulder and upper arm on the left side, be naked, to be admired. That suits you pale-skinned girls especially: when I see it, I want to kiss your shoulder, as far as it's shown.

女子要注重仪表

不认识的男子。这个，臂部摆动得合法，使她的长衫随风摇曳，尊贵地一步步向前走去。那个，像一个翁勃利[318]村夫的黄面婆一样，跨着大步走着。关于这一点，正如其他事情一样，应当有一个节度。这个太乡下气了，那个太柔软、太小心了。而且，你还得让肩头和左臂的上部都露出来。这事对于皮肤雪白的女人尤其适合，被这种情景所激动，我会渴望去吻我从那肩头所看到的一切。

Ⅶ: Learn Music and Read the Poets

The Sirens were sea-monsters, who, with singing voice, could restrain a ship's course as they wished. Ulysses, your body nearly melted hearing them, while the wax filled your companions' ears. Song is a thing of grace: girls, learn to sing: for many your voice is a better procuress than your looks. And repeat what you just heard in the marble theatre, and the latest songs played in the Egyptian style. No woman taught under my control should fail to know how to hold her lyre with the left hand, the plectrum with her right. Thracian Orpheus, with his lute, moved animals and stones, and Tartarus's lake and Cerberus, the tripleheaded hound.

海妖西兰们

7.学习音乐与阅读诗歌

西兰们[319]是海上的妖精，她们用悦耳的歌声把飞驶的船弄停了。西昔福斯的儿子[320]听了她们的歌声，几乎要把那缚住他的绳子弄断，而他的同伴们，幸亏那封住耳朵的蜡，才没有被诱惑。悦耳的歌声是一种迷人的东西，女子啊，学着唱歌吧(有许多面貌不美丽的女子是用声音来做诱惑方法的)。你们应当有时背诵那你们从云石的剧场里听来的曲子，有时唱着那带有独特节奏的尼罗河情歌。那些要向我请教的女子们不应该不懂得用右手握胡弓，左手拿箜篌的艺术。洛道迫山[321]的歌者奥尔弗斯[322]能用他的琴韵去感

At your song，Amphion，just avenger of your mother，the stones obligingly made Thebes's new walls. Though dumb，a Dolphin's thought to have responded to a human voice，as the tale of Arion's lyre noted. And learn to sweep both hands across the genial harpthat too is suitable for our sweet fun.

Let Callimachus，be known to you，Coan Philetas and the Teian Muse of old drunken Anacreon. And let Sappho be yours （well what's more wanton?），Menander，whose master's gulled by his Thracian slaves'

希腊诗人戴奥斯

动岩石、猛兽、鞑靼的湖和三头犬。你这个有正当理由替母亲复仇的人啊[323]，听了你的歌声，那些顽石很听话地前来搭成一座新的城墙。鱼虽然是哑的，但是却能够感受琴韵，假如你相信人们熟知的阿利洪[324]的故事。就学着用两手来弹古琴吧，这个欢快的乐器是有利于爱情的。

你们还应该知道加利马古思[325]、高司的诗人[326]和戴奥司的老人——酒的朋友[327]的诗歌。你们也得认识莎馥[328]（还有什么东西比她的诗更娇艳多情吗？）和那个描写被狡猾的葛达欺骗的父亲的诗人[329]。你也可以读一读那多情的泊洛拜尔谛乌思[330]，加鲁思[331]的或者是我们那可爱的谛蒲路思[332]的诗，或者是华鲁[333]所作的歌咏那使弗里若克思的妹妹[334]和那不幸的金毛公羊的诗。你们尤其应当读一读那歌咏流亡的艾耐阿斯——崇高

cunning and be able to recite tender Propertius's song, or some of yours Gallus or Tibullus; and the high-flown speech of Varro's fleece of golden wool, Phrixus, your sister Helle's lament; and Aeneas the wanderer, the beginnings of mighty Rome, than which there is no better known work in Latin. And perhaps my name will be mingled with those, my works not all given to Lethe's streams: and someone will say: "Read our master's cultured song, in which he teaches both the sexes; or choose from the three books stamped with the title Amores, that you recite softly with sweetly-teachable lips; or let your voice sing those letters he composed, the Heroides; he invented that form unknown to others." Oh grant it so, Phoebus! And, you, sacred powers of poetry, great horned Bacchus, and the Nine goddesses!

希腊女诗人莎馥

的罗马的建设者和行旅诗人的诗[335]，这是拉丁族最伟大的杰作。或许鄙人的贱名也可以附记于他们的鸿名之下，或许我的拙作不会被莱带河的水[336]所淹没。是的，或许有一个人会说："假如你真是一个有学问的女子，那么你就读一读我们老师开导男子两性的诗章[337]，或者在他所作的题名为《爱情》的三卷诗章中，选几节用你温柔而清脆的声音来念诗吧，或者，用一种轻盈的声调来念他《名人书简》中的一篇吧！"这种体裁在他以前是没有人知道的，他是发明者。斐菩斯，强有力的生着角的巴古斯，还有你们，贞洁的姊妹们，诗人的保护的神祇[338]，请倾听我的心愿吧！

Ⅷ：Learn Dancing，Games

Who doubts I'd wish a girl to know how to dance，and move her limbs as decreed when the wine goes round? The body's artistes，the theatre's spectacle，are loved：so great's the gracefulness of their agility. A few things shameful to mention，she must know how to callthe throws at knucklebones，and your values，you rolled dice：sometimes throwing three，sometimes thinking，closely，how to advance craftily，how to challenge. She should play the chess match warily not rashly，where one piece can be lost to two opponents，and a warrior wars without his companion who's been taken，and a rival often has to retrace the journey he began. Light spills should be poured from the open bag，nor should a spill be disturbed unless she can raise it. There's a kind of game，the board squared -off by as many lines，with precise calculation，as the

8.学习舞蹈和游戏

我愿意——这个别人是没有什么好怀疑的——女子能够跳舞，如果这样就应当在别人请求她跳舞的时候，她可以走出筵席来，优美地摆动着她的手臂。她的舞蹈使剧场中的看客皆大欢喜，这种优美的艺术对于我们来说是多么有蛊惑力的啊！我很惭愧说得这样琐细，可是我希望我的门徒能够精于掷骰子，而且一掷下去就会算出点数来，她应该有时掷出三点，有时恰巧掷出那可以赢的和所需要的点数来。我也希望我的门徒在下棋的时候不要吃败仗，一个“卒”是能够战胜两个敌人的，“王”是必须和“后”分开打仗的，一拼命，敌人就会逃跑。有一个赌法，按照那似水流年的月数划分，再密密地排列[339]。赌台每一面容纳三个棋子，谁第一个走到另一端谁就赢了[340]。千千万万的赌法都要熟练啊，一个女人不会赌博是可耻的，因为爱情往往是因为赌博而生出来的。可是把骰子掷得

fleeting year has months: a smaller board presents three stones each on either side where the winner will have made his line up together. There's a thousand games to be had: it's shameful for a girl not to know how to play; playing often brings on love. But there's not much labour in knowing all the moves: there's much more work in keeping to your rules. We're reckless, and revealed by eagerness itself, and in a game the naked heart's exposed. Anger enters, ugly mischief, desire for gain, quarrels and fights and anxious pain: accusations fly, the air echoes with shouts, and each calls on their outraged deities; there's no honour, they seek to cancel their debts at whim; and often I've seen cheeks wet with tears. Jupiter keep you free from all such vile reproaches, you who have any anxiety to please men.

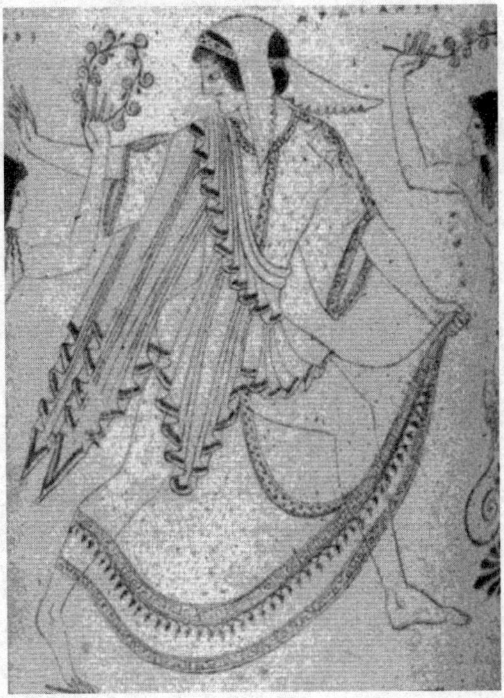

舞蹈的美女

很精也不是小事情啊，能够镇定是很重要的。在赌的时候我们往往会失于检点，火气把我们的性格暴露出来，而我们的心情也被别人赤裸裸地看穿了。生气、赢钱的心，笼罩着我们，因此便会发生口角、打架，和痛苦的遗憾。我们互相埋怨，口角声充满了空气，每个人都喊着神号互相骂着。在赌鬼那里，信用是没有的。为了赢钱，人们是什么心愿都敢许下的！我甚至经常看见那些满脸流着眼泪的人。想求爱的女子们，愿裘比德神为你们免了这些可耻的短处吧！

Ⅸ：Be Seen Around

Idle Nature has allotted these games to girls: men have more opportunity to play. Theirs the swift ball, the javelin and the hoop, and arms, and horses made to go in a circle. You have no Field of Mars, no ice-cold Aqua Virgo, you don't swim in the Tiber's calm waters. But it's fine to be seen out walking in the shade of Pompey's Porch when your head's on fire with Virgo's heavenly horses: visit the holy Palatine of laurel-wreathed Phoebus; he sank Cleopatra's galleys in the deep; the arcades Livia, Caesar's wife, and his sister, Octavia, started, and his son-in-law Agrippa's, crowned with naval

罗马执政庞培

9.经常抛头露面

女子啊，这些就是你们的优雅天性所允许你们的玩意儿，而男子们呢，他们的范围更大了。他们的玩意儿有网球、标枪、铁饼、武器和骑马。体育场是不合你们口味的，处女泉[341]冰冷的水也是不适合你们的。都斯古思平静的河水[342]，你们也不会去的。那你们可以的，而且对于你们有用的，就是当“太阳”的骏马跑进“处女宫”的时候[343]到庞培门下[344]去散散步。到巴拉丁山上戴月桂冠的斐菩斯的神殿里去巡礼一番——那个在海底把巴莱多尼恩[345]人的兵船弄沉的就是他——或者到“大帝”的妹妹和皇后，和他戴着海军王冠的女婿所建的建筑的纪念物[346]边上走走也好。为曼非斯的牝牛

honours; visit the incense-smoking altars of the Egyptian heifer, visit the three theatres, take some conspicuous seat; let the sand that's drenched with warm blood be seen, and the impetuous wheels rounding the turning-post. What's hidden is unknown: nothing unknown's desired; there's no prize for a face that truly lacks a witness. Though you excel Thamyras and Amoebeus in song, there's no great applause for an unknown lyre. If Apelles of Cos had never sculpted Venus, she'd be hidden, sunk beneath the waters. What do sacred poets seek but fame? It's the final goal of all our labours. Poets were once the concern of gods and kings: and the

脱拉岂阿诗人达米拉思

[347]献香烛的神坛下面也要去。以大出风头而闻名的三个戏院[348]尤其不可不去。那洒满热血的竞技场和转着飞奔马车的赛车场也要常去跑跑。隐藏者是始终不会为人所知的，不为人所知的人也就不会让人产生欲望。一张娇丽的脸儿，假如不让别人看到，那还有什么用呢？你唱，就可以超过达米拉思[349]和阿默勃思[350]，你的琴韵，假如不被别人听到，如何能够得到大名呢？假如那高司的画家阿贝莱思[351]不把他的“维纳斯画”展出来，这位女神恐怕到现在还沉没在大海吧！除了“不朽”，那些诗人的野心是什么呢？这是我们的工作所期待的最后目标。在过去，诗人是被神祇和国

ancient chorus earned a big reward. A bard's dignity was inviolable: his name was honoured, and he was often granted vast wealth. Ennius earned it, born in Calabria's hills, buried next to you, A great Scipio. Now the ivy wreaths lie without honour, and the painful toil of the learned Muses, in the night, has the name of idleness. But he's delighted to stay awake for fame: who'd know Homer, if his immortal work *the Iliad* were unknown? Who'd know of Danae, if she'd always been imprisoned, and lay hidden, an old woman, in her tower? Lovely girls, the crowd is useful to you. Often lift your feet above the threshold. The wolf shadows many sheep, to snatch just one, and Jupiter's eagle stoops on many birds. So

画家阿贝莱思

王所宠爱的，在古代他们的歌能够得到无数的回报，诗人的名字是神圣而受人尊敬的，而且人们往往给予他们无数的财富。伟大的思岂比奥[352]啊，那生在加拉勃里阿半岛山间的安钮思[353]被人认为应该葬在你的旁边。可是现在却斯文扫地了，对于缪赛们的勤劳也得到了一个“游手好闲”的名称。可是无论如何我们总是喜欢追名逐利的。假如那部不朽的杰作《伊里亚特》到现在还不为人所知，谁会认识荷马呢？假如达纳爱[354]老是深居在她的塔中，谁会认识她呢？她一定是无人知晓的，而且已经变成一个老太婆了。年轻的美人们啊，凑热闹是有用的。你们必须时常跑到外

too a lovely woman must let the people see her: and perhaps there'll be one among them she attracts. Keen to please she'll linger in all those places, and apply her whole mind to caring for her beauty. Chance rules everywhere: always dangle your bait; the fish will lurk in the least likely pool. Often hounds wander the wooded hills in vain, and the deer, un-driven, walks into the net. What was less hoped for by Andromeda, in chains, than that her tears could please anyone? Often a lover's found at a husband's funeral: walking with loosened hair and unchecked weeping suits you.

阿克修思达纳爱

面去。雌狼是要到大群的绵羊里找食物的；裘比德的鸟[355]是在有很多小鸟的田间翱翔的。美丽的女子也应该在人群中露脸:在人群中,她或许可以找到一个她可以诱惑的男子。她还要到处搔首弄姿,还应该注意一切能够增加美好的事物。机会到处都有,一直把持着你们的钓钩吧,那些你以为没有鱼的水里是肯定会有鱼的。猎狗在有很多树木的山上到处搜寻而一无所获是常有的事,人们并没有打猎,麋鹿却会自己投到罗网中来。那被绑在岩石上的昂德萝美黛[356]所希望的最后的事,不就是看自己的眼泪能够诱惑什么人吗？在自己丈夫被埋葬的时候找到另一个男子是常有的事。披头散发地走着,让自己的眼泪流着,这对于女人来说是再好看不过的了。

Ⅹ: Beware of False Lovers

Avoid those men who profess to looks and culture, who keep their hair carefully in place. What they tell you they've told a thousand girls: their love wanders and lingers in no one place. Woman, what can you do with a man more delicate than you, and one perhaps who has more lovers too? You'll scarcely credit it, but credit this: Troy would remain, if Cassandra's warnings had been heeded. Some will attack you with a lying pretence of love, and through that opening seek a shameful gain. But don't be tricked by hair gleaming with liquid nard, or short tongues pressed into their creases: don't be ensnared by a toga of finest threads, or that there's a ring on every finger. Per-

珈桑特拉

10.当心虚伪的情人

可是那些喜欢炫耀服饰和美丽，每根头发都有自己的位置的男子们，你们是应该置之不理的。他们对你们所说的话，他们早已向千千万万的女子说过了：他们的爱情是绝对靠不住的。一个女子，对于一个比自己还没有恒心，比自己还有更多情人的男子，有什么办法呢？这事你是不会相信的，可是你应该相信我。泊里阿摩思的女儿[357]啊，假如听了你的话，特洛伊城恐怕到现在也不会被攻破。有些男人戴着爱情的假面具来向女子钻营，他们只想从这条路上找到一些不要脸的猎物。不要被他们用松脂油涂在手指上的指环所诱惑。或许那穿得最漂亮的竟会是一个贼，想偷你华丽

haps the best dressed among them all's a thief, and burns with love of your finery. "Give it me back!" the girl who's robbed will often cry, "Give it me back!" At the top of her voice in the cattle-market. Venus, from your temple, all glittering with gold, you calmly watch the quarrel, and you, Appian nymphs. There are names known for a certain sort of reputation too, they're guilty of deceiving many lovers. Learn from other's grief to fear your own: don't let the door be opened to lying men. Athenian girls, beware of trusting Theseus's oaths: those gods he calls to witness,

凯克洛泊斯

的衣饰。"把我的东西还给我啊!"这就是被骗的女子们时常喊着的。整个公堂都回荡着这种呼声:"把我的东西还给我啊!"维纳斯啊,你们的邻家女子阿比阿丝[358]啊,你们一点也不感动地从你们金碧辉煌的庙上俯视着这些纠葛。除了那些窃贼以外,还有那些著名的淫棍,被他们欺骗的女人,免不了要分担他们的恶名。前车可鉴,你们的门永远不应当让一个诱惑者进来。凯克洛泊斯的女儿们[359]啊,不要相信戴设斯的誓言,这不是他第一次对着神祇发誓啊!而你,岱莫冯,戴设斯的薄幸的继承人,在欺骗过菲丽丝[360]以后,已没有人相信你了。假如你们的情人嘴上说得很好听,

he's called on before. And you, Demophoon, heir to Theseus's crimes, no honour remains to you, with Phyllis left behind. If they promise truly, promise in as many words: and if they give, you give the joys that were agreed. She might as well put out the sleepless Vestal's fire, and snatch the holy relics from your Temple, Ino, and give her man hemlock and monkshood crushed together, as deny him sex if she's received his gifts.

罗马家神薇丝达

那么你们就也像他们一样满口只说好听的就是了，假如他们拿东西送给你们，你们也要用相当的情谊回答他们，一个女子是能够熄灭薇丝达[361]永远燃烧的火，掠取伊纳古思[362]女儿神祠里的圣物，和献毒酒给丈夫喝的，假如收了情夫的礼物怎能不把爱的狂欢给他呢！

Ⅺ: Take Care with Letters

Let me speak closer to the theme: hold the reins, Muses, don't smash the wheels with galloping. His letters written on fir-wood tablets test the waters: make sure a suitable servant receives the message. Consider it: and read what, gathered from his own words, he said, and perhaps, from its intent, what he might anxiously be asking. And wait a little while before you answer: waiting always arouses love, if it's only for a short time. But don't give in too easily to a young man's prayers, nor yet deny him what he seeks out of cruelty. Make him fear and hope together, every time you write, let hope seem more certain and fear grow less. Write elegantly girls, but in neutral ordinary words, an everyday sort of style pleases. Ah! How often a doubting lover's been set on fire by letters, and good looks have been harmed by barbarous words! But since, though you

11.认真对待信件

可是我不会越说越远，缪赛，勒住你的骏马吧，不要越出范围。用一封信札前来探路，一个伶俐的侍女收下了它，小心地念着它，信上所用的语气足够使你辨得出那些表白的心愿是否真诚，是否出于迷恋的心。不要立刻就复信。等待，只要不是很长久，就能够把爱情弄得格外热烈。对于一个年轻情郎的请求，你要摆出一些架子，可是也不要一口回绝。要弄得他心惊肉跳，同时也要给他希望，要用每一封回信逐渐地坚定他的希望，减少他的害怕。女子们所用的词句应当是简洁而亲切的，平常谈话的口气是再可爱不过的了。多少次啊，一封信燃起了游移在一颗心里的情焰！多少次啊，一种不通顺的词句毁坏了美的幻影！可是，既然不戴贞洁的假面具，要欺骗你们的丈夫而不使他们起疑，你们就需要有一个谨慎的侍女或是奴隶来为你们传递书简，年轻而没有经验的奴仆是万万靠不

lack the marriage ribbons, it's your concern to deceive your lovers, write the tablets in your maid's or boy's hand, don't trust these tokens to a new young man. He who keeps such tokens is treacherous, but nevertheless he holds the flames of Etna. I've seen girls, made pallid by this terror, submit to slavery, poor things, for many years. I judge that countering fraud with fraud's allowed, the law lets arms be wielded against arms. One form's used in exercising many hands, (Ah!Perish those that give me reason for this warning) don't write again on wax unless it's all been scraped, lest the single tablet contain two hands. And always speak of your lover as female when you write: let it be "her" in your letters, instead of "him".

掌管文艺的缪赛女神

住的。毫无疑问的,那个掌握这种把柄的人是没有良心的,可是他所拥有的兵器比艾特纳[363]山的雷霆还要厉害啊!我看见无数的女子,为了这种不谨慎,害怕得脸儿发青,吃了一辈子的亏。在我想来,我们可以用欺骗来回答欺骗,而法律也允许以兵器攻击兵器,你们需要有能够用一只手写出几种笔迹来的本领(啊!那些使我逼不得已教你们采取这种方法的人,你们死去吧),不先把字迹擦去再复信的人真是傻子,信札上留着两个人的手迹。当你们作书给你们情郎的时候,你需要用写给你们女友的口气,在你的信上,要称"他"的地方都要改称"她"。

Ⅻ：Avoid the Vices，Favour the Poets

If I might turn from lesser to greater things，and spread the full expanse of swelling sail，it's important to banish looks of anger from your face：bright peace suits human beings，anger the wild beast. Anger swells the face：the veins darken with blood：the eyes flash more savagely than the Gorgon's."Away with you，flute，you're not worth all that." said Pallas when she saw her face in the water. You too if you looked in the mirror in your anger，that girl would scarcely know her own face. Pride does no less harm to your looks：love is attracted to friendly eyes. We hate (believe the expert) extravagant disdain：a silent face often sows the seeds of our dislike. Glance at a glance，smile tenderly at a smile：he nods，you too return the signal you received. When he's practised，so，the boy leaves the foils，and takes his sharp arrows from his quiver. We hate sad

12.用艺术陶冶情操，远离恶习

我们暂且把这些琐事放在一边而说那些重要的事情。为了让你们的颜面好看，你们必须把你们的脾气忍住而不要释放出来。心平气和是合乎人类本性的，就像暴怒是合乎猛兽的一样。一发怒，脸便会板起来，黑血把脉络也涨粗了，而在眼睛里，高尔戈[364]一切的火都燃烧起来了。"走开，你这可恶的笛子，你不值得让我为你牺牲我的美。"葩拉丝在水里看见了自己的影子便这样说[365]。你们也是如此，在你们盛怒的时候，假如你们去照一照镜子，恐怕没有一个人会认得出那是你自己的脸来。骄傲也会破坏你们的美丽，要勾起爱情，就要媚眼儿。相信我的经验吧，太骄傲的神气是我们所憎厌的。往往即使是一句话都不说，脸上也会带着恨的根苗。有人注视你，那么你也注视他。有人向你温柔地微笑，你也要向他温柔地微笑。假如有人向你点头，你也向他打个招呼，阿谟尔也是先用钝

girls too: let Ajax choose Tecmessa: a happy girl charms us cheerful people. I'd never ask you, Andromache, or you, Tecmessawhile there's another lover for me than you. I find it hard to believe, though I'm forced to by your children, that you ever slept with your husbands. Do you suppose that gloomy wife ever said to Ajax: "Light of my life"; or the words that usually delight a man?

Who'll prevent me using great examples for little things, why should

笛子的发明者葩拉丝

箭尝试,然后再从箭囊里拔出利箭来的。我们也憎恨悲哀。让黛克梅莎去被阿约思爱吧,像我们这种快乐的民族,一个快乐的女子才能够撩动我们的春心。不,绝对不是盎特罗玛黑,绝对不是黛克梅莎,你们两个人,我不想让你们的任何一个来做我的情妇。我甚至还不大相信,虽然你们的子孙使我不得不相信,你们会和你们的丈夫同床。一个沉浸在悲哀中的女人,怎么会对阿约思说"我的生命啊",这是一切男子听到了都会全身舒畅的话。

we be afraid of the leader's name? Our good leader trusts those commanders with a squad, these with the cavalry, that man to guard the standard. You too should judge what each of us is good for, and place each one in his proper role. The rich give gifts: the lawyer appears as promised: often he pleads a client's case that must be heard. We who make songs, can only send you songs: we are the choir here best suited above all to love. We can make beauties that please us widely known: Nemesis has a name, and Cynthia has; you'll have heard of Lycoris from East to West; and many ask who my Corinna is. Add that guile is absent from the sacred poets, and our art too fashions our characters. Ambition and desire for possession don't touch us: the shady couch is cherished, the forum scorned. But we're easily caught, torn by powerful passions, and we know too well how to love with perfect faith. No doubt our minds are sweetened by gentle art, and our natures are consistent with our studies. Girls, be kind to the poets of Helicon: there's divinity in them, and they're the

请允许我为我无足轻重的艺术引用几个伟大的艺术的例子，而且请允许我把这艺术和统兵大元帅的企图来作一个比拟。一位精明的大元帅会把一百个步兵的统带权托付给一个将官，把一队骑兵托付给另外一个将官，把旗卫兵再托付给一个将官。你们也是如此，你们需要审察一下，我们中的某个人做某件事是合适的，是对你们有用的。让有钱的人送礼物，让法学家出主意，让律师打官司，我们这些做诗的人呢，让我们做诗送给你们，我们这一群人比什么人都更懂得恋爱，我们会让那些我们迷恋的美人名闻遐迩。奈梅西丝[366]出名了，卿蒂阿[367]也出名了，自西至东，丽高里丝[368]的名字谁都知道了，而且人们也时常问起我所讴歌的高丽娜[369]是谁。我还要说，那些诗人，神圣的人物，有一颗不知道"负心"的心，而我们的艺术又用它的意象把我们改造过了。我们是既不会为野心，也不会为金钱所摇动的；我们厌恶名利，只要阴暗和一张卧榻就满足了[370]。我们是很容易结识的，我们长久地烧着热烈的情火，我们知道用真心真意去爱。毫无疑问，我们的性格已经受到和平的艺术陶冶，而我们的习惯

Muses' friends. There's a god in us, and our dealings are with the heavens: this inspiration comes from ethereal heights. It's a sin to hope for gifts from the poet: ah me! No girl's afraid of that sin. Still hide it, don't look greedy at first sight: new love will balk when it sees the snare.

水边的美女

也和我们的努力同化了。年轻的美人啊，对于诗人们，鲍艾沃帝阿的神祇[371]的弟子，我们身上附着神明，而我们又和天有交往，我们的灵感是从天上降下来的。博学的诗人等待金钱是一种罪恶。啊！这是一种任何女子都害怕的罪恶。女人啊，你们至少要学会矫饰，不要一下子就把你们贪婪的心暴露出来，一看见是陷阱，一个新的情郎就要被吓跑了。

XⅢ: Try Young and Older Lovers

No rider rules a horse that's lately known the reins, with the same bit as one that's truly mastered, nor will the same way serve to captivate the mind of mature years and of green youth. This raw recruit, first known of now in love's campaigns, who reaches your threshold, a fresh prize, must know you only, always cling to you alone: this crop must be surrounded by high hedges. Keep rivals away: you'll win while you hold just one; love and power don't last long when they're shared. Your older warrior loves sensibly and wisely, suffers much that the beginner won't endure: he won't break the door down, burn it with cruel fire, attack his mistress's tender cheeks with his nails, or rip apart his clothing or his girl's, nor will torn hair be a cause of tears. That suits hot boys, the time of strong desire: but he'll bear cruel wounds with calm mind. He burns, alas, with

13.年老的情人与年轻的情人

一个老练的马夫使用辔头,对于新马和对于旧马是有所不同的。同一个理由,为了引诱一颗有经验的心和一个青春的少年,你们不应该采取同样的方法。那个被你准许进入你卧房里的,第一次进入情场的新手、新的猎物,应该让他只知道你,应该使他老是在你的旁边,这是应该四周围着篱笆的植物。你需要提防着情敌,只要你对他不放松警惕,你就一定能够胜利了,维纳斯的权力,就像国王的权力一样,一旦离开就会糟糕。至于另外一个,那个老兵,会神不知鬼不觉地,乖乖地爱着,他能忍受许多新兵所无法忍受的事情。他不会打破你们的门或者是烧你们的门,他不会用他的指甲抓破他情妇的嫩脸,他不会撕破她的长衣或是一个女子的衣服,而且,对于他,即使马被劫去了他也不会流眼泪的。那激情是一个在青春期和恋爱期中的少年所仅有的。而另外一个呢,他会耐心地忍

slow fires, like wet straw, like new-cut timber on the mountain height. This love's more sure: that's brief and more prolific; snatch the swift fruits, that fly, in your hand.

丛林中的维纳斯

受着那些最厉害的伤痛。他所燃烧的情火是不旺的。啊！就像正在燃烧的湿稻草，或者是刚从山上砍下来的柴一样。这种爱情是靠得住的，而那种爱情虽然热烈，但是却不能长久，快点去采那瞬间即逝的昙花吧！

XⅣ: Use Jealousy and Fear

Let all be betrayed; I've unbarred the gates to the enemy: and let my loyalty be to treacherous betrayal. What's easily given nourishes love poorly: mingle the odd rejection with welcome fun. Let him lie before the door, crying: "Cruel entrance!" pleading very humbly, threatening a lot too. We can't stand sweetness: bitterness renews our taste; often a yacht sinks swamped by a favourable wind; this is what bitter wives can't endure; their husbands can come to them when they wish; add a closed door and a hard-mouthed janitor, saying: "You can't." And love will touch you too. Drop the blunted foils now: fight with blades; no doubt I'll be attacked with my own weapons. Also when the lover you've just caught falls into the net, let him think that only he has access to your room. Later let him sense a rival, the bed's shared pact: remove these arts, and love

14.运用嫉妒与恐惧

我就要把一切献给敌人[372]了(我们早就开门临敌了),而对于我的叛逆,我也存着一颗至诚不欺的心。太容易垂青是很难长久培养爱情的,在温柔的欢乐中应该夹入一些拒绝。让你的情郎站在门口,要让他叫着"忍心的门"!要使他不停地哀求和威吓。清淡的东西是我们所不欢喜的,一种苦的饮料倒能够打开我们的胃口。一只船被顺风打翻沉没是常有的事。下面是阻碍一个丈夫爱自己妻子的理由:无论什么时候,想要看她就能够看见她。把你的门关起来吧,叫你的守门人对他说:"不许进来。"一旦被关在门外,爱情便会热烈起来了!现在把钝的兵器抛下拿起锋利的兵器吧!我相信就要看见我给你们的箭反而要向我射来了。当一个新的情郎坠入你的情网时,你要让他一开始暗自庆幸能独尝禁脔,不久你便要给他一个你其实是另有所钟,而你的思念并非他所独得的恐惧。假如

grows old. The horse runs swiftly from the starting gate, when he has others to pass, and others follow. Wrongs relight the dying fires, as you wish: See (I confess!), I don't love unless I'm hurt. Still, don't give cause for grief, excessively, let the anxious man suspect it, rather than know. Stir him with a dismal watchman, fictitiously set to guard you, and the excessively irksome care of a harsh husband. Pleasure that comes with safety's less enjoyable: though you're freer than Thais, pretend fear. Though the door's easier, let him in at the window, and show signs of fear

热恋中的神女

没有这种战略,爱情便会老去。一匹骏马只有在对手超过它的时候或者是要赶上它的时候才会拼命奔跑的。假如我们的情焰熄灭了,是要用妒忌来使它重新燃起的。对于我来说,我承认如果别人不伤害我,我是不会爱的。可是不要让你的情郎明白他苦痛的原因,要让他提心吊胆,不知道到底是怎么一回事。你要骗他说有一个奴隶在暗地里留心你们的一举一动,一个很厉害的丈夫在想尽办法捉奸,这样才能够使爱情兴奋。没有危险,欢乐也就没有劲了。即使你是比达伊丝[373],非常自由自在,你也会疑神疑鬼地害怕。当你可以很容易让你的情郎从门里进来的时候,你就偏

on your face. A clever maid should leap up and cry:"We're lost!" You, hide the trembling youth in any hole. Still safe loving should be mixed with fright, lest he consider you hardly worth a night.

爱的火焰

要让他从窗口爬进来，而且你的脸儿也需要装出惊恐的表情。需要有一个狡猾的侍女急急忙忙地跑进来，喊着："我们糟了！"于是，你便把你那个吓得浑身发抖的少年情郎随便放在哪里去藏一藏。可是，在这恐惧之后，你要让他安逸地尝一尝维纳斯欢乐的异味，不要让他太吃亏。

XV：Play Cloak and Dagger

I nearly forgot the skilful ways by which you can elude a husband，or a vigilant guardian. Let the bride fear her husband：to guard a wife is right；it's fitting，it's decreed by law，the courts，and modesty. But for you too be guarded，scarcely released from prison，who could bear it? Adhere to my religion，and deceive! Though as many eyes as Argus owned observe you，you'll deceive them（if only your will is firm）. How can a guard make sure that you can't write，when you're given all that time to spend washing? When a knowing maid can carry letters you've penned，concealed in the deep curves of her warm breasts? When she can hide papers fastened to her calf，or bear charming notes tied beneath her feet? The guard's on the look-out for that，your go-between offers her back as paper，and takes your words on her flesh. Also a letter's safe，and

15.掩饰和耍花招

如何瞒过一个狡猾的丈夫或者是一个尽职尽责的看守人，我差一点忘记讲了。我希望一个妻子害怕他的丈夫，我希望她是被看守得好好的，这是在礼仪上所推崇，在法律上、正义上、贞操上所坚守的。可是你，刚被裁判官用小棒触着而获得解放的女奴[374]，谁能给你同样的监守呢？你到我的学校里来听听如何欺骗的课程吧！那些监视的人，即使他们有和阿尔古司[375]一样多的眼睛，只要你有决心，你就一定能够把他们一个个都瞒过了。当你一个人洗澡的时候，一个监守人如何能够妨碍你写信呢？假使你让你同谋的侍女把情书放在她的胸脯边或鞋底里，监守人如何能够妨碍她送出去呢？可是假如那监守人已经看穿了这个把戏，那么你就要让你的同谋露出她的背来，把情书写在皮肤上。一个可以瞒过别人眼睛最靠得住的方法，就是用新挤的牛乳来写信，只要用些炭末一撒，字就清

deceives the eye, written with fresh milk; you read it by scattering it with crushed ashes. And those traced out with a point wetted with linseed oil, so that the empty tablet carries secret messages. Acrisius took care to imprison his daughter, Danae: but she still made him a grandfather by her sin. What good's a guard, with so many theatres in the city, when she's free to gaze at horses paired together, when she sits occupied with the Egyptian heifer's sistrum, and goes where male companions cannot go, when male eyes are banned from Bona Dea's temple, except those she

有一百双眼睛的阿尔古司

清楚楚地显现了。用亚麻茎中挤出来的液体书写也有同样的效果,于是那不容易引起别人怀疑的信札上其实有着别人所看不见的字。阿克里修思亲自小心地看管着他的女儿[376],可是她终究还是犯了奸,请他做了外祖父。在罗马有那么多的戏院,她有时去看赛车,有时去看赛会,当她到那些她的监守人不能进去的地方(因为善良女神[377]是不准男子们走进她的神祠去的,那些她高兴让他们进去的男子是例外)时,当那可怜的监守

orders to enter? When, with the girls' clothes guarded by a servant at the door, the baths conceal so many secret joys, when, however many times she's needed, a friend feigns illness, and however ill she is can leave her bed, when the false key tells by its name what we should do, and the door alone doesn't grant the exits you seek? And the jailor's attention's fuddled with much wine, even though the grapes were picked on Spanish hills: then there are drugs that bring deep sleep, and close eyes overcome

阿尔哥斯的国王阿克里修斯

人在那藏着胆大的情郎的浴池外看守着女子的衣裳时，一个监守人如何能够管住女子呢？在必要的时候，她难道不能找到一个口里嚷着生病的女友（口说生病，却把自己的床让给她）？那个名叫“奸情女”[378]的复制的钥匙不是已经为我们指出应该怎么办了吗？而且要到情妇的房间里去，我们难道非得从门里进去不可吗？为了躲开监守人的监视，我们还可以用黎阿葛士的液体[379]，西班牙山上出产的也可以。还有一种能叫人深深睡去的药，它能够使一个莱带河[380]的夜压在别人的眼睛上。还有一种幸

by Lethe's night; or your maid can rightly detain the wretch with lengthy games, and be associated herself with long delays. But why use these tortuous ways and minor rules, when the least gift will buy a guardian? Believe me gifts captivate men and gods: Jupiter himself is pleased with the gifts he's given. What can the wise man do, when the fool love's gifts? He'll be silent too when a gift's accepted. But let the guard be bought for once and all: who surrenders to it once, will surrender often.

I remember I lamented, friends are to be feared: that complaint's not only true of men. If you're credulous, others snatch your joys, and that hare you started running goes to others. She too, who eagerly offers room and bed, believe me, she's been mine more than once. Don't let too beautiful a maid serve you: she's often offered herself to me as my lady.

福的战略，就是让你同谋的侍女用欢乐的香饵迷住那个可憎的监守人，让她用千般温柔长长久久地留住他。可是如果只需要一点小小的回报就能够贿赂那个监守人，我们又何必来转许多弯，婉转曲折地去想法子呢？用礼物，你们要相信我啊，不论是人还是神都会被诱惑的，就是裘比德大神也会上祭祀物的当。所以不论是聪明人还是笨人，礼物是没有人不喜欢的，即使是丈夫，当他收到礼物的时候，也会装聋作哑的。可是你只要每年收买他一次就足够了，他伸过一次手，自己也就会时常伸手的。

我曾经有过遗憾，我想起来了，朋友是不可信任的[381]，这个遗憾不仅仅是对男子们来说的。假如你太信任他人，其他女子就要来分享你爱情欢乐的甜蜜了，而你可以得到的兔子，也要被别人弄去了。即使是那个肯把自己的房间和床借给你的忠实的朋友[382]，听我的话吧，她也和我有过好多次关系。不要用太漂亮的女仆，她会常常在我这儿取得她主人的地位。

XⅥ: Make Him Believe He's Loved

What am I talking of, madman? Why show a naked front to the enemy, and betray myself on my own evidence? The bird doesn't show the hunter where to find it, the stag doesn't teach the savage hounds to run. Let others seek advantage: faithful to how I started, I'll go on. I'll give the Lemnian girls swords to kill me. Make us believe (it's so easy) that we're loved: faith comes easily to the loving in their prayers. Let a woman look longingly at her young man, sigh deeply, and ask him why he comes so late: add tears, and feigned grief over a rival, and tear at his cheeks with her nails: he'll straight away be convinced; and she'll be pitied, and he'll say: "She's seized by love of me." Especially if he's cultured, pleased with his mirror, he'll believe he could touch the goddesses with love. But you, whatever wrong occurs, be lightly troubled, nor in poor

16.让他相信你是爱他的

我要把自己弄成什么样啊,我这傻子?为什么袒着胸去迎接敌人呢?为什么要自己出卖自己呢?鸟是不会把捕捉自己的方法告诉捕鸟人的,鹿是不会把自己逃走的路指给那将要扑到它身上去的猎犬看的。我自己有什么好处呢?可是不要去管他,我大大方方地继续着我的企图,把那可以将我置于死地的兵器给予兰诺司的女子们[383]。你们需要让我们自以为是被爱着的(而且这是很容易的事),热情很容易坚信它所冀望的一切。女子只要向年轻的男子瞟一瞟情眼、深深地叹息,或者问他为什么来得这样迟就够了。你们还要加上眼泪,一种矫作的妒忌的愤怒,再用你们的指甲抓碎他的脸,他就会立刻坚信不疑了,他便会对你一往情深了。他将会说:"她发狂地爱着我。"尤其是那些漂亮的、常常照镜子的,自以为能打动女神的心的花花公子。可是无论如何,假如受到了冒犯,你们千万不

spirits if you hear of a rival.

Don't believe too quickly: how quick belief can wound, Peocris should be an example to you. There's a sacred fountain, and sweet green-turfed ground, near to the bright slopes of flowered Hymettus; the low woods form a grove; strawberry-trees touch the grass, it smells of rosemary, bay and black myrtle: there's no lack of foliage, dense box and fragile tamarisk, nor fine clover, and cultivated pine. The many kinds of leaves and grass-heads tremble at the touch of light winds and refreshing breezes. Thequiet pleased Cephalus: leaving men and dogs behind, theweary youth often

凯发路思

要把不高兴表现得太露骨，知道你的情郎另外还有一个情妇，你也千万不要气得发昏！

而且不要轻易地相信，太轻易相信是多么的危险啊！泊洛克丽丝[384]已经给了你们一个证明的例子。在那繁花似锦含笑的希买多斯山[385]旁，有一个圣泉，一片绿茵遮住了土地。矮矮的树木形成了一片森林，杨梅树荫庇着碧草，迷迭香、月桂、翠绿的番石榴薰香了空气，在那边还有许多枝叶茂密的黄杨树、袅娜的西河柳、金雀花和苍松。在和煦的微风中，一切树叶和草都微微地颤动着。凯发路思[386]是喜欢安静的，离开了仆役和犬，这个疲

set– tled on this spot，“Come，fickle breeze（Aura），who cools my heat” he used to sing，“be welcome to my breast.” Some officious person，evilly remembering what he'd heard，brought it to the wife's fearful hearing. Procris，as she took the name Aura to be some rival，fainted，and was suddenly dumb with grief. She grew pale，as the leaves of choice vine–stalks grow pale，wounded by an early winter，or ripe quinces arching on their branches，or cornelian cherries not yet fit for us to eat. As her breath returned，she tore the thin clothing from her breast，and scratched at her innocent cheeks with her nails. Then she fled quickly，frenzied，down the ways，hair flowing，like a Maenad roused by the thyrsus. As she came near，she left her companions in the valley，bravely herself entered the grove，in secret，on silent feet. What was in your mind，when you hid there so foolishly，Procris? What ardour，in your terrified heart? Did you think she'd come soon，Aura，whoever she was，and her infamy be visible to your eyes. Now regretting that you came（not wishing to surprise them）now

倦的年轻人常常到那个地方去闲坐。他总是这样唱:“飘忽不定的凉风啊，到我心头平息我的怒火吧!”有人听到这几句话，记住了，轻轻地告诉他那提心吊胆的妻子。当泊洛克丽丝知道了这个她以为是情敌的“凉风”的名字后，她便昏了过去，痛苦得连话都说不出来了。她的脸色变成了惨白，就像那被初冬的寒气所侵袭的、采摘了葡萄的葡萄叶，或是那累累垂挂在枝头的、已经成熟的启道奈阿的果实[387]，如同那还没有熟透的阳桃一样惨白。当她清醒过来的时候，她把自己胸前的轻衫撕破，又用指甲把自己的脸儿抓破——这张脸儿是经不起这种待遇的。随后又突然披散着头发，狂怒着，她在路上奔跑着，好像被巴古斯的松球杖所激动了一样。到了那听说的地方时，她把她的女伴留在谷中，她急忙躲躲藏藏、蹑手蹑脚地走进树林。泊洛克丽丝，这样鬼鬼祟祟的，你的计划是什么啊?什么热焰燃起了你那迷塞的心啊?你无疑是想着那个“凉风”，那个你所不认识的“凉风”就要来了，而你又将亲眼看见奸情。有时你非常懊悔来到这里，因为你不愿意惊散他们，有时你自言自语，你的爱情不知道该如何决

pleased: doubting love twists at your heart. The place, the name, the witness, command belief, and the mind always thinks what it fears is true. She saw signs that a body had pressed down the grass, her chest throbbed, quivering with its anxious heart. Now noon had contracted the thin shadows, and dawn and twilight were parted equally: behold, Cephalus, Hermes's child, returned to the wood, and plunged his burning face in the fountain's water. You hid, Procris, anxiously; he lay down as usual on the grass, and cried: "Come you zephyrs, you sweet air (Aura)!" As her joyous error in the name came to the miserable girl, her wits and the true colour of her face returned. She rose, and with agitated body moved the opposing leaves, a wife running to her husband's arms. He, sure a wild beast moved, leapt youthfully to his feet, grasping his spear in his right hand. What are you doing, unhappy man? That's no creature, hold back your throw! Alas, your girl's pierced by your spear! She called out: "Ah me! You've pierced a loving heart. That part always takes its wound from

定,使你的心不停地跳动。你用地点、人名、告密人,和那多情的男子容易和人发生恋爱的可能性来作你盲信的辩解。在被压倒的草上一看见有一个生物的足迹,她的心便立刻狂跳起来。太阳已经到了中午时分,已经把影子缩短了,它悬在天的正中。这时那个岂莱耐山神祇[388]的后裔凯发路思回到了树林里,他用泉水浇着自己被晒热的脸。泊洛克丽丝,你害怕地躲着,而他却躺在那块常常躺的草地上,嘴里说着:"温柔的和风,你来啊,而你,凉风,你也来啊!"那个不幸的泊洛克丽丝快乐地发现了那个由于一句模棱两可的话而引起的错误,她安心了,她的脸色也恢复了原状。她站了起来,那女子想要冲到她丈夫的怀里去,因此她便翻动了那拦在路上的树叶。凯发路思以为是一头野兽来了,他便用一个少年人的敏捷身手拿起了他的弓,箭已经握在他的右手中了。不幸的人,你要做什么啊?这不是野兽,留住你的箭吧!箭已射中了你的妻子。"哎哟!"她喊着,"你射穿了一颗爱你的心。这颗总是被凯发路思所伤的心。我是在不该死的时候死了,可是我却没有情敌。大地啊,当你掩盖我的时候,我感觉轻

Cephalus. I die before my time, but not wounded by a rival: that will ensure you, earth, lie lightly on me. Now my spirit departs into that air with its deceptive name: I pass, I go, dear hand, close my eyes!" He held the body of his dying lady on his sad breast, and bathed the cruel wound with his tears. She died, and her breath, passing little by little from her rash breast, was caught on her sad lover's lips.

谋尔古虑思

松了许多。那个引起我误会的'凉风'已经把我生命的气息带走了。我死了。哦!亲爱的用你的手把我的眼皮合下吧!"他呢,陷入深深的悲哀,将那占有了他心灵的人儿的垂死的娇躯放在臂弯;他的泪水洒在那残酷的伤痕上。可是一切全完了,那轻信谣言的泊洛克丽丝的灵魂已经渐渐从她的胸头离去,而凯发路思,把他的嘴唇贴在她的嘴唇上,吸取了她最后的呼吸。

XⅦ: Watch How You Eat and Drink

But to resume the work: bare facts for me so that my weary vessel can reach harbour. You're anxiously expecting, while I lead you to dinner, that you can even ask for my advice there too. Come late, and come upon us charmingly in the lamplight: you'll come with pleasing delay; delay's a grand seductress. Even if you're plain, with drink you'll seem beautiful, and night itself grants concealment to your failings. Take the food daintily: how you eat does matter; don't smear your face all over with a greasy hand. Don't eat before at home, but stop before you're full: be a little less eager than you can be; if Paris, Priam's son, saw Helen eating greedily, he'd detest it, and say: "Mine's a foolish prize." It's more fitting, and it suits girls more, to drink; Bacchus you don't go badly with Venus's boy. So long as the head holds out, and the mind and feet stand

17.赴宴时应有的表现

不多赘言,言归正传。我不应该委婉曲折地说下去,我那已经疲倦的船快要进港了。你不耐烦地等着我领你到宴会去,而且还想让我教你关于赴宴的规则。你应该去得很迟,而且你的姿态也不该在灯还没有亮之前显露出来,等待能够增加你的身价,除了等待之外没有其他更好的撮合人了。假如你很丑,那么在喝醉了的人的眼里也是美丽的,而且夜也足够掩饰住你的缺陷了。用你的指头撮取菜肴[389],吃得好看也是一种艺术,不要用没有拭干净的手去抹你的脸。在赴宴之前不要先在家里吃,可是在筵席上,却不能够吃得太饱,要留一点儿胃口。假如泊里阿摩思的儿子[390] 看见海伦拼命地大喝大嚼,他准会说:"我得到了一个多么傻的胜利啊!"喝适量的酒对于女子来说是适宜的,维纳斯的儿子和巴古斯混在一起是很和谐的。可是你的头应当能够承受那些酒,不要让你的机敏和行

firm: and you don't see two of what's only one. Shameful a woman lying there, drenched with too much wine: she's worthy of sleeping with anyone who'll have her. And it's not safe to fall asleep at table: many shameful things usually happen in sleep.

宴会中的女子

为被弄昏,不要让你的眼睛发花了。一个女子喝得酩酊大醉躺在地上,那是一个多么难看的奇怪现象啊!随便一个人就可以得到她。在筵席上一瞌睡就要有危险,瞌睡是冒犯贞操的好机会。

ⅩⅧ：And So To Bed

To have been taught more is shameful; but kindly Venus said: “What's shameful is my particular concern.” Let each girl know herself: adopt a reliable posture for her body; one layout's not suitable for all. She who's known for her face, lie there face upwards: let her back be seen, she who's back delights. Milanion bore Atalanta's legs on his shoulders: if they're good looking, that mode's acceptable. Let the small be carried by a horse; Andromache, his Theban bride, was too tall to straddle Hector's horse. Let a woman noted for her length of body, press the bed with her knees, arch her neck slightly. She who has youthful thighs, and faultless breasts, the man might stand, she spread, with her body downwards. Don't think it shameful to loosen your hair, like a Maenad, and throw back your head with its flowing tresses. You too, whom Lucina's marked with

18.床榻的温馨

我很害羞讲下去，可是那好第奥奈[391]对我说：“你所害羞的正是我们的事业。”每个女子都需要认识自己，按照你的体格，你可以选择各种各样的姿势，同样的姿态不能够适合所有的女子。那脸蛋儿特别漂亮的女子应当仰卧着。那些满意自己臂部的要把自己的臂部显露出来。露岂娜[392]曾经遗留下一些皱纹在你的肚子上吗？那么，你也要像巴尔底人一样，反转了背脊交战。米拉尼洪把阿达良达的腿放在自己的肩上，假如你的腿是美丽的，你便要照样搁上去。矮小的女子应当采取骑士的姿势，身子很长的皎白女子[393]——海克笃尔的妻子，从不跨在她丈夫的身上，像跨在一匹马上一样。身体颀长的女子要跪在床上，头稍向后弯。假如你的腿股拥有青春的娇媚可爱，而你的胸膛也是完美的，那么男子应该直立着，而你便斜斜地躺在床上。采取这种姿势的时候，不要怕羞。你要把你

childbirth's wrinkles, like the swift child of Parthia, turn your mount around. There's a thousand ways to do it: simple and least effort, is just to lie there half-turned on your right side. But neither Phoebus's tripods nor Ammon's horn shall sing greater truths to you than my Muse. If you trust art's promise, that I've long employed: my songs will offer you their promise. Woman, feel love, melted to your very bones, and let both delight equally in the thing. Don't leave out seductive coos and delightful murmurings, don't let wild words be silent in the middle of your games. You too whom nature denies sexual feeling, pretend to sweet delight with artful sounds. Unhappy girl, for whom that sluggish place is numb, which man and woman equally should enjoy. Only beware when you feign it, lest it shows: create belief in your movements

三脚的椅子

的头发披散开,像跳神的女子那样,而且转着头飘散着你的头发。品尝维纳斯的欢乐有千姿百态,最简单而最不吃力的方法就是半身侧卧在右面。可是那斐菩斯的三脚椅[394],和生着牛头的阿孟[395]都不能比我的缪赛给你更可靠的启示,假如我的话有几句是值得相信的,那么你们便接受我的教导吧,这是一个长久经验的结果,我的诗是不会欺骗你们的。女子啊,我愿维纳斯的欢乐一直透进你的骨髓里,也愿你和你的情郎分享那种快乐!情话和琐语永远不要间断,而在你们的肉搏中,猥亵的话是应该夹进去的。即使像你这种老天吝于赐给爱情的幽欢感觉的人,你也要假装着,用温柔的谎话,说你是能够感觉到那种幽欢的。那种生着麻木的能给男女以快感

and your eyes. When you like it, show it with cries and panting breath. Ah! I blush, that part has its own secret signs. She who asks fondly for a gift after love's delights, can't want her request to carry any weight. Don't let light into the room through all the windows: it's fitting for much of your body to be concealed.

The game is done: time to descend. You swans, you who bent your necks beneath my yoke. As once the boys, so now my crowd of girls inscribe on your trophies "Ovid was my master."

利比阿的神祇阿孟

器官的女子，是多么可怜啊！可是这种矫饰千万不要被发现；要使你的动作和你的眼神能够帮助你来欺骗我们！放荡、软语、喘息能够给人一种幻觉。我讲下去也有一点儿害羞了，这个器官也有它自己秘密的表情。在维纳斯的幽欢之后去向情郎要求赠物，那是不需要费力恳求的。我忘记说了：在卧房里不要让光线从窗子透进来；你身体的好多部分是不能在日光下被人看见的。

我的废话已经讲完了：现在已经是走下那天鹅驾着的车子的时候了[396]。就像从前的男子一样，现在女子，我的女弟子，在她们的战利品上这样写着："奥维德是我们的老师。"

注释索引

Contents of footnote

(1)Amor,爱情之神,或称柯毗陀 Cupido,就是希腊神话里的爱卢斯 Eros,是维纳斯,即希腊神话里的阿孚罗谛特 Aphrodite 的儿子,形象为一个小孩子,生有翅膀,手执弓矢。

(2)Automedon,阿岂赖斯的御人。

(3)Tiphys,是约松 Iason 坐着去取金羊毛的阿尔戈船 Argo 的舵工。

(4)指阿尔戈船,它是用带沙利阿 Thessalia 的贝利翁山 Pelion 的树木建造的,带沙利阿旧名为海木尼阿 Haemonia,因此这样称呼。

(5)Venus,掌管恋爱的女神。

(6)Philyra,是岂龙 Chiron 的母亲。

(7)Achilles,希腊英雄,《伊里亚特》中的名将。

(8)Hector,《伊里亚特》中的名将,特洛伊人中最勇敢的,后来被阿岂赖斯所杀。

(9)Aeacus,是阿岂赖斯的祖父。

(10)阿谟尔是维纳斯之子,阿岂赖斯是黛蒂丝 Thetis 之子。

(11)Phoebus,即阿波罗 Apollo,日神,文艺之神。

(12)Ascra,古希腊大诗人海西沃度斯 Hesiodus 的故乡。

(13)Clio,九位文艺女神之一,掌管历史。

(14)指九位缪赛(文艺女神)。

(15)这种轻盈的细带只有没嫁人的处女才可以佩戴,奴隶、异国人,或者刚从奴隶身份中解放出来的女子是不能佩戴的。

(16)这是一种罩在衣衫上的、一直遮到脚上的长衣,只有罗马的贵妇人可以穿。

(17)在罗马,如果对方不是奴隶、异国人,或是解放了的奴隶,和有夫之妇发生关系是很危险的。犯了奸淫的人要被人从屋顶掷到地上或者是鞭笞至死。

(18)Perseus,是主神裘比德 Juppiter,即希腊神话中的宙斯 Zeus 之子,在杀了怪物梅度沙 Medusa 之后, 他乘了梅度沙的血变成的飞马贝迦苏斯 Ppegasus 来到艾帝活比阿国 Aethiopia。在那里,国王凯绅斯 Cepheus 为了要消除海怪的骚扰,将他的女儿昂德萝美黛来献祭,拜尔塞斯杀了海怪,便娶了昂德萝美黛。

(19)Andromeda,见前条。

(20)弗里基阿人,指巴黎斯 Paris,事迹见《伊里亚特》。

(21)希腊女子,指海伦 Helena,事迹见《伊里亚特》。

(22)Gargara,米西阿 Mysia 的伊达山 Ida 的最高峰和它下面的城镇的名字。

(23)Methymna,是赖斯步司 Lesbos 中的一个镇。

(24)Aeneas,是维纳斯的儿子,罗马人的先祖。

(25)七月。

(26)Pompeius(公元前107~公元前48年),罗马大将第一次三头政治的执政之一。

(27)指屋大维门和与它毗连的马尔凯卢斯剧场;马尔凯卢斯Marcellus是屋大维Octaria的儿子。

(28)Livia(纪元前56~纪元后59年)。奥格斯特Augustus之妻。

(29)培鲁斯Belus的孙女们,即达那乌斯Danaus的女儿们,一共有五十个,她们除了幼女西拜尔纳丝特拉Hypermnestra外,都受她们的父亲达那乌斯的指使,在新婚之夜中杀了她们的新郎,就是她们的堂兄弟。

(30)见前条。

(31)指巴拉丁山Palatium上的阿普罗廊庑。

(32)Adonis,是一个美丽的少年,维纳斯的爱人,被野猪所伤而死。为了纪念他的死,每年人民在城中排班游行,抬着一个吊床,上面放着阿陶尼斯的蜡像,并盖满了花,女人们则唱哀歌,到了早晨这蜡像就被投到海里。

(33)指伊西丝Isis,埃及的繁殖女神,有时画作牛首人身。就等于希腊神话中的伊沃Io,被裘比德所恋,海拉Hera妒忌她,将她变作一头母牛。

(34)Appias,一群水妖,维纳斯神殿前的雕像。

(35)Romulus,传说是罗马的建设者和第一个国王,曾吩咐他的部下在一个大型庆祝活动中抢劫沙皮尼人的妇女为妻。

(36)Sabini,意大利的古民族。

(37)赛神会的行列在竞技场的游艺开始时,从裘比德的神殿出来,穿过市场和牲口市场,然后到竞技场来,在场中绕了一个圈子。神祇的像被放在车中,或者是在肩舆上。

(38)指Caesar Octauius Augustus(公元前63~公元14年)是Gaius Julius Caesar(公元前102~公元前44年)的侄儿。

(39)凯克洛泊斯Cecrops,传说是雅典的创立者,"凯克洛泊斯的儿郎"就是指雅典人。

(40)指希腊舰队在爱琴海打败波斯舰队那件事。

(41)Parthi,古民族之一,罗马人的敌人,时常来骚扰罗马。

(42)Crassus(公元前115~公元前53年),罗马大将,第一次三头政治的执政之一,被巴尔底人谋杀。

(43)指凯乌斯·恺撒Caius Caesar,绰号"小兵靴"。Caligula,是奥格斯特的曾孙,当时只有20岁,是一个很有作为的人,等到做了国王后,他立刻变成了一个疯狂的暴君,"让他们恨我,但是让他们怕我""Oderint,dum metuant",这是他对臣仆的态度,后来被自己的臣仆谋杀。

(44)谛伦斯Tiryns,是海尔古赖斯Hercules的家乡,谛伦斯的英雄就是指海尔古赖斯。他小时候在摇篮中扼死了两条大蛇,那是裘娜Juno,即希腊神话中的Hera,是被派遣来害死他的。

(45)Bacchus,酒神。希腊神话说他曾经被裘娜追逐,漫游各地。他的旅程中最著名的是远征印度,据说经过很长时间,胜利而回。

(46)酒神巴古斯的手杖,杖端是一个松球,缠绕着葡萄蔓和常春藤。

(47)指凯乌斯·恺撒。见注(43)。

(48)指巴尔底的王——弗拉特五世 Phraste,他杀掉父亲奥洛特 Orode 而篡位。

(49)Latium,罗马所在的地方。

(50)Mars,战神。

(51)凯旋者披着的 Toga Piota 是绛红色且缀着金星的。

(52)Euphrates,亚洲西部的一条河,出源于亚美尼亚,接连底格里斯 Tigris 河,流入波斯湾。

(53)Armenia,亚洲西部地名。

(54)Danae,波斯开国人,启路斯 Cyrus 是她的子孙。

(55)Achaemenes,是启路斯的祖父,阿凯曼耐斯的子孙即波斯人。

(56)三位女神是:维纳斯、裘娜和阿黛那 Athena。在柏勒斯 Peleus 和黛蒂丝结婚时,大宴诸神,唯独没有请掌管不和的女神艾里斯 Eris,艾里斯大怒,将一个上面刻着"给最美的人"字样的金苹果投在席上,于是维纳斯、裘娜、阿黛那三位女神便相争这个金苹果,因为她们都认为自己是最美丽的人。主神宙斯让她们到巴黎斯面前,由他评定谁最美。巴黎斯评定维纳斯最美,因为她让他得到最美丽的妻子,后来巴黎斯航海到希腊诱得海伦,因为她,后来就发生了特洛伊战争。

(57)Baiac,是在纳泊尔湾中的一个城,以矿泉而著名。罗马人在那里修建了华丽的浴场。

(58)第阿娜 Diana,是罗马神话中的月神和狩猎女神,是一个独身女神,即希腊神话里的亚耳台米思 Artemis。她的神殿在阿利启阿 Aricia,离罗马城 25 公里的拉丁姆小城,在阿尔巴奴思山下,一个名叫第阿娜镜 Specu lum Dianae 的湖畔。神殿的祭司名叫"树林之王"Rex Nemorensis,要得到祭师之职,必须要杀死前任祭师。

(59)Thalia,九位文艺女神之一,掌管喜剧和牧歌。"不平衡的车轮"是指悲歌的两章而言。

(60)Maenalus,是阿尔迦第阿 Arcadia 的一座山名。

(61)Byblis,是一个水仙,爱着她的哥哥迦奴思 Cannus,徒劳地追逐他经过许多地方,最终自缢而死,化作一道泉水。见奥维德的《变形记》。

(62)Myrrha,她的父亲是岂尼拉思 Cinyras。这件不幸的事是维纳斯的报复在作祟。见奥维德的《变形记》。

(63)Ida,克来特的山名。

(64)Cnossos,克来特名城。

(65)Cydonia,克来特北部名城。

(66)Pasiphae,米诺思之后。

(67)Crete,一小岛名。

(68)Minos,克来特之王。

(69)指巴古斯,因为他的母亲守梅娄 Semele 是住在鲍艾沃帝阿 Boeotia 的都城带白 Thebae 的;鲍艾沃帝阿旧名为阿沃尼阿 Aonia,因此这样说。

(70)Bacohae,庆祝巴古斯节日的巫女。她们奔跑着,披散头发,戴着常春藤冠,手中拿着松球,跳着舞,狂喊着。

(71)Europa,裘比德爱上了她,变成了一头可爱的白牛,走到她身边,弯下身体,欧罗巴骑在它身上,裘比德便背着她到克来特去,在那里他们生了三个孩子。

(72)Io,见注(33)。

(73)指米诺多思路 Minotaurus,是葩西法艾和一头牛所生的半牛半人的怪物,后来被戴设斯 Theseus 所杀。

(74)指阿艾罗泊 Aerope,米诺思的孙女,阿特拉思 Atreus 的妻子。

(75)Thyestes,阿特拉思的弟弟。

(76)指丝启拉 Scylla,是尼须思 Nisus 的女儿。她割去她父亲头上的系着命运和生命的头发给米诺思——她的爱人,她父亲的敌人,后被变作一个腰上长着许多恶狗的怪物,或说被从船上投到海中,变作一只永远作为海鹰的猎品的小鸟。

(77)指阿迦曼农 Agamemnon,特洛伊战役中希腊军的主将,回国后被他不忠诚的妻子克丽黛纳思特拉 Clytaemnestra 和她的情夫艾纪思都思 Aegisthus 所谋杀。

(78)Neptunus,海神,等于希腊神话中的 Poseidon。

(79)Ephyra,高林都思的古名,是希腊的一座城。

(80)Creusa,高林都思的公主,约松的妻子。

(81)指美黛阿 Medea,约松的前妻,她是一个魔女。她帮助约松去采金羊毛,后来约松爱上了克莱乌莎,她很嫉妒,送了一个匣子给克莱乌莎,这匣子飞出火来烧死了克莱乌莎。并且,美黛阿把自己和约松所生的孩子也杀死。

(82)斐尼克思 Phoenix,是 Amyntor 的儿子,被阿明托尔的妾所诬陷,被阿明托尔挖去了眼睛。

(83)Hippolytus,是戴设斯的儿子。当戴设斯和弗特拉 Phaedra 结婚后,弗特拉爱上了他前妻的儿子伊包里度思,但是他却拒绝了她的要求。于是她因为失望和怨恨而自缢,留下了一卷对伊包里度思的诬蔑信给她的丈夫。这受骗的丈夫看了十分气愤,要求海神奈泊都诺思为他报仇。一天,伊包里度思驾车到海边去,海上忽然出现了一头海怪,他的马大惊,将车子撞翻,伊包里度思因此而死。

(84)Phineus,他听了他后妻的谗言,弄死了他的儿子们,后来裘比德降罪于他,使他瞎了眼,而且每次有食物时,都被哈尔比艾 Harpyiae(意为掠夺者),一种半鸟半妇人的怪物抢去。

(85)屋里赛思,他用木马藏兵计攻陷了特洛伊城。

(86)指维纳斯节,在4月1日,紧接着3月。3月在拉丁文是 Martius,是从马尔斯 Mars 变出来的。马尔斯是维纳斯的爱慕者之一。

(87)Pleiades,七星,这里是指七星消失不见的时候,11月8~11日,时常会有风暴。

(88)指十月初。

(89)Allia,拉丁姆的一条河,纪元前389年,罗马人在那里被迦里阿人Gallia打败。

(90)Priamus,海克笃尔之父,事迹见《伊里亚特》。

(91)Cydippe,是一个雅典女子,在她的脚下,阿工谛乌思Acontius掷了一个苹果,上面写着:“我向亚耳台米思Artemis宣誓,我将嫁给阿工谛乌思。”绮第珮高声宣读,于是被女神作为阿工谛乌思的质言。

(92)Penelope,是屋里赛思Ulysses的妻子,以贞洁坚忍而出名,事见《奥特赛》。

(93)Pergamus,特洛伊的城塞。

(94)在拟曲中,少女的角色是男子扮的。

(95)Cybeleius,是弗里基阿Phrygia的一座山的名字;启倍莱虞斯山的女神,是启倍莱Cybele,为弗里基阿人的女神,后来被罗马人所崇拜,她的教士是被阉割过的。

(96)指阿丽亚特娜Ariadna,是米诺思和葩西法艾的女儿,帮助戴设斯杀死米诺多路思[见注(73),后被戴设斯所弃,遂为巴古斯所恋]。

(97)见注(83)。

(98)女神指维纳斯,见注(32)。

(99)Liber,是古意大利的一位神祇,后来和希腊神话中的巴古斯相混,此处指巴古斯。

(100)指阿丽亚特娜[见注(96)],因为住在格诺苏斯,因此这样说。

(101)Dia,是格诺苏斯对面的一个小岛。

(102)Mimallonides,是跳神诸女[见注(70)]的别称。

(103)Satyrs,是巴古斯的伴侣,头发竖起,两只尖的耳朵长在头上,额上生着两只小角,脚像羊脚一样;手里拿着一只酒杯,或者一支松球杖,或者一个乐器。

(104)Silenus,巴古斯的保护者和随从,秃顶,骑驴,老是喝醉。

(105)指巴古斯。

(106)Euhius(Evius),巴古斯的别名;曷荷艾(euhoe)是跳神诸女的欢呼声,是从Euhius这个字变化出来的。

(107)指巴古斯。

(108)Eurytion,是一个半人半马的怪物。在比里都思Pirithous和阿脱勒思Atreus之女希芭达米亚Hippodamia结婚的时候,半人半马的怪物们也是宾客,其中艾里谛洪想对新娘无礼,因此决斗而死。见《变形记》第十二卷。

(109) 葩拉丝Pallas,希腊神话里的智慧女神,即罗马神话中的米奈尔伐Minerva,如同希腊神话中的阿黛那。弗里基阿树林在伊达山上,见注(63)。

(110)孔雀。

(111)Aeolus,风的主宰。

(112)Styx,是冥土中一条河的名字,诸神祇对着它发誓。

(113)Thrasius,是一个神明的启泊鲁斯岛人。

(114)Busiris,古埃及的国王,以残忍出名。

(115)Phalaris,耶稣纪元6世纪前的阿格里干顿国的暴君。

(116)Perillus,是一个雅典的金匠,为法拉里思铸了一头铜牛,犯罪的人就被关在这铜牛中烧死,培里鲁思是第一个被烧死的。

(117)Phoebe,不是日神斐菩斯的妹妹,而是另外一个Phoebe,她的妹妹是希拉伊拉 Hilaira。她们的父亲勒启布思 Leacipus 将她们许给伊达思 ldas 和林开思 Lynceus 的兄弟。迦思笃尔 Castor 和保鲁克思 Pollus 迷恋着她们,将她们抢去。事见奥维德的《年代纪》。

(118) 指思凯洛斯岛 Sclus 的利高美代思王 Lycomedes 的女儿黛伊达米亚 Deidamia。

(119)指阿岂赖斯。阿岂赖斯的母亲黛蒂丝预知她儿子不幸的未来,所以让他扮作一个女子,送他到思凯洛斯岛利高美代思的王宫里,和公主们在一起,在那里他和黛伊达米亚发生了关系。后来屋里赛思去找他,扮作一个商人,在一个篮子里放了许多妇人的饰物和一柄剑去献给利高美代思的女儿们,她们都来取饰物,而阿岂赖斯则是取了剑,于是屋里赛思毫不费力地找到了他,让他加入特洛伊战役。

(120)指维纳斯。参见注(56)。

(121)指巴黎斯。参见注(56)。

(122)Llion,即特洛伊城。

(123)指海伦之夫美奈拉乌思 Menelaus。

(124)见注(119)。

(125)即阿岂赖斯,参见注(9)。

(126)葩拉丝也是战争女神。

(127)指阿岂赖斯的长矛。那支长矛是启洪送给阿岂赖斯的父亲柏勒斯的,后来传给阿岂赖斯。

(128)指黛伊达米亚。

(129)Orion,奈泊都诺思之子,是一个巨大的猎人,容貌英俊,被第阿娜变成一颗星星。

(130)Side,未详。

(131)Daphnis,谋尔古卢思 Mercurius 之子,是一个牧人,田园诗歌的创造者,被一个水仙所爱,她让他发誓永远忠于她,背誓就会变成盲人。

(132)Pirithous,弗特拉的丈夫戴设斯的密友。

(133)Pylades,是奥莱思代思 Orestes 的至友。

(134)Hermione,是海伦之女,奥莱思代思之妻。

(135)Tyndareus,斯巴达的王,他的女儿是海伦,迦思笃尔和保鲁克思是和她一胎生的。

(136)Proteus,是一个海神,能变作各种形状。

(137)Iopaean,是颂阿普罗的欢乐歌。

(138)指古希腊大诗人海西沃度斯。见注(12)。

(139)指荷马 Homerus,传说梅奥尼阿 Maeonla 是他的故乡。

(140)Amyclae,斯巴达东南方的一座城。

(141)指海伦,事见《伊里亚特》。

(142)指巴黎斯。

(143)另一个希苞达迷亚,是希苞达米亚的祖母[见注(108)]。这里的希苞达米亚是屋伊诺冒思 Oenomaus 的女儿。一个预言说只有能赛车胜过她父亲的人才能娶她为妻。后来贝洛迫思 Pelops 爱上了她,和她的父亲赛车,她贿赂她父亲的御人,去掉了她父亲车轮的车辐,贝洛迫思于是获胜。

(144)指贝洛迫思。

(145)指维纳斯,因岂带拉岛 Cythera 是供奉维纳斯的。

(146)指柯毗陀,维纳斯之子。

(147)Erato,是九位文艺女神之一,司爱情诗歌,她的名字在希腊文是 Erato,和希腊文的 eran(恋爱)是同一语根。

(148)指代达鲁思 Daedalus,是一个雅典的著名建筑师,他为米诺思建造了一座迷宫,关住米诺思的妻子葩西法艾和一头牛所生的半牛半人的怪物米诺多路思。后来他得罪了米诺思,便被监禁了。代达鲁思便为他的儿子伊迦鲁思 Icarus 和自己各造了两个翅膀,从空中脱逃。但是他的儿子飞得太高,翼上的蜡被太阳所熔,便坠海而死。他死的地方,后人称做伊迦里姆海 Icarium,是爱琴海的一部分。

(149)见注(112)。

(150)指迦丽丝陀 Callisto,代格阿 Tagea 国王利迦翁 Lycaon 的女儿,被裘娜变成一头熊,裘比德将她变成一颗星星,即大熊星。

(151)Bootes,一颗星名。

(152)Samos,爱琴海中的岛名。

(153)Naxus,爱琴海中岛名。

(154)Paros,爱琴海中岛名。

(155)Delos,爱琴海中岛名,在那里有阿美国罗的神殿;克拉里乌思 Clarius,是阿普罗的别名。

(156)Lebinthos,爱琴海中的岛名。

(157)Calymne,爱琴海中的岛名。

(158)Astypalaea,爱琴海中的岛名。

(159)指阿谟尔。

(160)海木尼阿,是带沙利阿的古名,那儿的女子被人视为巫女。

(161)一种生在小马额上的瘤,被人视为一种春药。

(162)Medea,见注(81)。

(163)Marsi,是意大利的古民族,以春药及巫术闻名,时见于诗人歌咏中。

(164)指美黛阿；法西斯 Phasis，是高尔岂斯 Colchis，美黛阿家乡的一条河。

(165)指约松[见注(81)]。Aeson 是他的父亲。

(166)Circe，是一个具有魔法的女神，恋着屋里赛思，她和屋里赛思的事迹见《奥特赛》。

(167)Nireus，在特洛伊战役中，希腊英雄中的最美丽者。

(168)Hylas，一个美丽的少年，在米西阿 Mysia 为拿牙黛丝们(水妖)所偷去。代奥克里都思 Theocritus 的牧歌第八首上就讲这事。

(169)指希腊文和拉丁文。

(170)指启尔凯和珈丽泊苏。

(171)Calypso，水神，奥尔底季阿岛 Ortygia 的女王，她救了遇难的屋里赛思，爱上了他，在岛中留了他七年才放他回去。见《奥特赛》。

(172)指雷梭斯 Thesus，是脱拉岂阿 Thracia 的国王，奥特里赛人 Odrysac 就是脱拉岂阿人。

(173)Simois，特洛伊的小河名。

(174)Dolon，特洛伊的善走者，夜到希腊营侦探，途遇屋里赛思，被他所杀。见《伊思亚特》。

(175)指阿岂赖斯，因为他生于带沙利阿之夫底阿城 Phtia；带沙利阿旧名为海木尼亚，因此这样说。

(176)Sithonius，即脱拉岂阿人。雷梭思是来帮助特洛伊人的。一个预言曾说，假如雷梭思的马吃到了特洛伊人的牧草，希腊人便不能攻下特洛伊城，所以第沃麦代思 Diomedes 和屋里赛思偷了他的马，并且杀死了他。

(177)指鸽子，在艾比路斯 Epirus 的道道尼阿附近，有一座圣林，林中有一座裘比德的神殿，那儿的鸽子用人语启示神意。卡屋尼阿 Chaonia 是艾比路斯的一部分，因此这样说。

(178)见注(41)。

(179)Numidia，是北阿非利加洲的一个地名。

(180)Atalanta，是阿尔迦第阿国王，美丽，善竞走。她拒绝向她求婚的少年，说："先和我赛跑，胜则娶我，败则处死。"后来一个美少年米拉尼洪 Milanion，或称希包买奈思 Hipomenes，得到维纳斯的帮助，胜了阿达朗达，便和她结婚。诺那克里阿人 Nonacrian，即阿尔迦第阿人，因为诺那克里阿是阿尔迦第阿北方的一个城。

(181)指米拉尼洪。

(182)指阿达朗达。

(183)Hylaeus，是一个半人半马的怪物，被阿达朗达所杀。

(184)指爱神柯毗陀的箭。

(185)见注(60)。

(186)指海尔古赖斯[见注(44)]，是裘比德和阿尔克曼娜 Alcmena 所生的儿子。他一生下时裘比德的妻子裘娜就恨他，想弄死他，但没有成功。后来她知道不能害他，便决定让他冒许多险，一生得不到平安快乐。蔼里思特思 Eurystheus 让他做的十二件大工作，就是裘娜嫉恨的结果，但是海尔古赖斯却都做成了。第十一件大工作是取金苹果，当承负天空的盎达蔼思 Antaeus 替他去取金苹果时，他为他背负天空。

(187)见注(44)。

(188)指阿普罗。阿普罗杀死了岂克罗伯师 Cyclops，被裘比德贬到人间，为阿特美都思王牧牛一年。肯丢斯 Cynthius 是代罗斯 Delos 岛上的山名，那儿是阿普罗的出生地。

(189)Admetus，带沙利阿的费雷 Pherae 的统治者。

(190)即阿普罗。

(191)Leandrus，是一个美少年，爱上了赛斯都斯 Sestos 的维纳斯的女司祭海罗 Hero，海罗答应他在夜里到她那里，清晨回去。有一天，风浪很大，他依然游泳去和她约会，被水溺死。

(192)6 月 24 日。传说是罗马开国后的第六个国王 Servius Tullius 为幸运之神 Fortuna 建立神殿的日子。Servius 是从 Servus(奴隶之子)变化出来的。

(193)7 月 7 日。在迦里阿人退了之后，罗马邻近的民族(并不是迦里阿人)，通知罗马的元老院，让他们把全罗马的自由妇女都献给他们。元老们听了一个女仆的计策，让罗马的女仆都穿上了她们女主人的衣服到敌人的营里去，把他们灌醉了。然后罗马人出兵，于是大获全胜。因此 7 月 7 日是“女仆节”。

(194)果子铺是在圣路上。

(195)Amaryllis，是田园诗歌中一个美丽的牧女。

(196)此句典出维尔吉留思 Virgilius 的《牧歌》*Eclogo* 第二章：lpse cgo cana legam tenera lanugine mala，Casaneasque nuces，mca quas Amaryllis amabat。意为：“我亲自采了那有柔毛的白色野木瓜，和我的阿马里力思所爱的栗子。”

(197)Tyrus，是福艾尼开 Phoenice 的一个地名，以出产绛色而出名。

(198)Cos，爱琴海中的一个岛。

(199)是三个高尔戈 Gorgon 之一，起初容貌非常美，有美丽的头发，后来触怒了米奈尔伐女神，米奈尔伐将她的头发变成可怕的蛇，她的眼睛一旦看到别人，那人就会变成顽石，后来被拜尔塞斯所杀。

(200)见注(201)

(201)Phyllis，是希腊传说中的脱拉岂阿国王西东 Sithon 的女儿，戴设斯之子岱莫冯的未婚妻。岱莫冯在约定的时间不回来和她结婚，她自缢而死。

(202)见注(92)。

(203)见注(92)。

(204)Laodamia，泊洛代西拉乌思之妻。

(205) 指泊洛代西拉乌思 Protesilaus，特洛伊战役中希腊军队到特洛伊的第一人，为海克笃尔所杀。费拉古思 Phylacus 是他的祖父。

(206)指巴黎斯。

(207)指美奈拉乌思，阿特拉思是他的父亲。

(208)指巴古斯，见注(69)，他的角是不可抵抗的力的象征。

(209)见注(81)。

(210)指阿特拉思之子阿迦曼农，见注(95)。

(211)指克丽黛纳思特拉。

(212)Chryses，是阿普罗神的一个祭司。

(213)指勃丽赛伊丝 Briseis，利尔奈索斯 Lyrnesos 是特洛伊的一个镇，是她的出生地。

(214)希腊军队围特洛伊城，在四周进行掠夺，阿普罗的祭司克里赛司的女儿克里赛伊思 Chryseis 被掳去做阿迦曼农的侍妾，祭司祈求阿普罗神，神便降瘟疫给希腊军队。阿岂赖斯因此和阿迦曼农在议席上起了冲突。后来阿迦曼农放了祭司的女儿，把阿岂赖斯喜欢的女子勃丽赛丝夺来，阿岂赖斯大怒，退出了战场。事迹见《伊里亚特》。

(215)指珈桑特拉 Cassandra，特洛伊城被攻，珈桑特拉就成了阿迦曼农的女奴，可是一到希腊，便被迦阿迦曼农的妻子杀害。

(216)指克丽黛纳思特拉。

(217)指艾幻思都思。Thyestes 是他的父亲。

(218)Eryx，是 Sicilia 岛中的一座山名。那儿有一座有名的维纳斯庙。

(219)Alcathous，贝洛迫思之子，希腊的美迦拉 Megara 城的重建者，此处指美迦拉城。

(220)Hymettus，是非洲的一座山名，以蜜蜂及云石闻名。

(221)Boreas，北风。

(222)Eurus，东南风。

(223)Zephyrus，温暖的西风。

(224)Notus，南风。

(225)Machaon，是医药神艾思古拉比乌思 Aesulapius 之子，是一个著名的医师。

(226)这句在希腊文中是：Gnothi Seauton。

(227)Athos，迦尔岂斯半岛边上的一座山。

(228)Hybla，是 Sicilia 岛的一座山，以蜜蜂命名。

(229)指橄榄树。

(230)因为他是从筵席上回来，所以戴着蔷薇花冠。

(231)是求爱的表示，有时把花挂在门上。

(232)指艾比路斯的道道尼阿的橡树，那些橡树据说会启示神意。

(233)Olympia。诸神的居处。

(234)Vulcanus，罗马神话里的火神。即希腊神话里的海弗思都思 Hephaestus。

(235)Lemnos，在那儿胡尔迦奴思最受人崇拜。

(236)马尔斯的居处。

(237)Paphos,那里的人是崇拜维纳斯的。

(238)Dione,维纳斯之母,此处引申作维纳斯解。

(239)Ceres,罗马的农事女神。

(240)Samothrace,爱琴海上的一个岛,在那里,人们第一个祀奉着迦皮里 Cabiri。

(241)Tantalus,是一个国王,因为泄露了诸神会议的秘密(或说为了把自己儿子贝洛迫思的肉给诸神吃),所以罚他站在一个湖的中央,水一直浸到他的头边,但他要喝水的时候,水就退了;他头上垂挂着极好的果子,但他要去采的时候,果子就避开了。

(242)Cytherea,即维纳斯,见注(145)。

(243)因为她是艾帝沃比阿人,所以颜色是棕色的。见注(18)。

(244)指拜尔塞斯。见注(18)。

(245)Andromache,海克笃尔之妻。

(246)Illyria,意大利东面对岸的一块多山的区域。

(247)维纳斯的目光是游移的。

(248)米奈尔伐的眼睛是青黄色的。

(249)见注(11)。

(250)海伦之女。见注(134)。

(251)Gorge,阿尔黛阿 Althaea 之女。

(252)指勃丽赛伊丝。见注(213)。

(253)柘榴是维纳斯的树。

(254)Podalirius,是医药神艾思古拉比乌思之子,是一个希腊的名医。

(255)见注(9)。

(256)Nestor,特洛伊战役希腊军中最老最有经验的人。

(257)Calchas,特洛伊战役希腊军中的占卜者。

(258)Telamon,特洛伊战役中希腊英雄阿约思 Ajax 之父。

(259)见注(2)。

(260)阿岂赖斯的至友巴特洛格鲁思借他的甲盾去和海克笃尔战斗,被海尔笃尔所杀。阿岂赖斯听见至友已死,甲盾丧失,既悲且怒,他的母亲为他求天上的铁匠胡尔迦怒思为他一夜之间打造了甲胄兵器,后来终于杀死了海克笃尔。

(261)Amaxones,传说是一个善战的女子民族,她们养了男孩就丢掉,而且自己烧去左乳,以便弯弓。

(262)Penthesilea,阿尔逊人的女王,特洛伊战役中特洛伊人的联盟,被阿岂赖斯所杀。

(263)指维纳斯。

(264)指阿谟尔。

(265)指美奈拉乌思和阿迦曼农。

(266)指克丽黛纳思特拉。见注(77)。

(267)Talaus,乘阿尔戈船远征中的一人。

(268)Eriphyla,盎非阿拉乌思之妻。

(269)指盎非阿拉乌思 Amphiaraus,是奥伊克歇思 Oecleus 之子,攻带白城 Thebae 七英雄之一,明知此战必死,匿而不出,因为他是一个预言者。但他曾允许他的妻子爱丽菲拉,凡他自己和首领特拉斯都思 Adrastus 有意见不同处,便取决于他的妻子。保里尼凯思 Polynices,同征者之一,乃以哈尔穆宜亚 Harmnia 的项圈贿赂爱丽菲拉,她于是主张出征。结果,当他在沿河奔逃的时候,裘比德让大地裂开,盎非阿拉乌思与他的车马陷入地里。

(270)指冥土。

(271)指泊洛代西拉乌思。见注(205)。

(272)指拉奥达米阿。见注(204)。

(273)指阿尔开丝黛 Alcestis。她的丈夫阿特美都思病得快要死的时候,命运女神们说假如有人肯代替他死,他便能活。阿尔开丝黛便去替代他。后为洛洛赛尔比娜 Proserpina(或云海尔古赖斯)自冥土携回。

(274)指阿特美都思。费莱思 Pheres 是他的父亲。

(275)Capaneus,攻带白城七英雄之一,其妻为曷阿德芮。当加巴纳思被裘比德以雷击死后行葬礼时,她投入骨灰内,以身殉夫。

(276)Iphias,伊非思 Iphis 之女,即曷阿德芮 Evadne,加巴纳思之妻。

(277)指美黛阿。见注(81)。

(278)指约松。

(279)指克莱乌莎。见注(80)。

(280)见注(96)。

(281)见注(201)。

(282)Elissa,即第多 Dido,迦太基女王。在维尔吉留思的 Aeneis 里说,她殷勤地款待特洛伊亡命的英雄艾耐阿斯,而且爱上了他,但后来艾耐阿斯膺神意他去,不得不离开了她,她便以宝剑自杀于火葬堆上。

(283)指维纳斯。见注(145)。

(284)指海伦,代拉泊奈 Therapne 是她的出生地。

(285)指古希腊诗人施岱西阿鲁思 Stesichorus。“Stesikhoros 歌咏 Ilion 事,于 Helene 有微词,已而病目,疑为祟。且考核史迹,也以旧说为诞。因作反歌(Palinedia),言 Helene 未尝至 Ilion,其实是 Zeus 派遣了一个化身(Eidolon)代之往也,未畿疾瘳……”(以上抄自周作人著《欧洲文学史》)。

(286)Endymion,是一个美丽的牧人,为月神第阿娜所爱,她把他带到拉特摩司山上,害怕他老了变丑了,便设法使他永远睡着。

(287)Latmus,在卡利阿 Caria。

(288)Cephalus,是一个年轻的猎人,奥洛拉爱着他,将他抢了去,但他始终爱着他的妻子泊洛克丽丝 Procris。

(289)指黎明女神奥洛拉 Aurora。

(290) 艾耐阿斯是维纳斯和盎启赛思 Anchises 所生的儿子，哈尔穆宜阿 Harmonia 是维纳斯和马尔斯所生的女儿。

(291)指维纳斯。伊达良 Idalium 是启泊鲁斯的城名，在那儿，她特别为人们所崇拜。

(292)指海克笃尔。

(293)Capitolium，供奉裘比德的神殿，建立在罗马 Mons Tarpejus(达尔贝于斯山)上。

(294)Tatius，沙皮尼族的王，和罗摩路斯同治罗马。

(295)指王宫 Domus Augustana(奥格斯特家)，内有一个阿普罗神殿。

(296)见注(228)。

(297)Alps，欧洲西南部山脉。

(298)Iole，奥哈里阿 Oechalia 国王曷里都思 Eurytus 的女儿。

(299)指阿丽亚特娜。见注(96)。

(300)格尔马奈 Germanae 族人用某种草来染发，而迦里阿人，据恺撒在《记事》第五卷上说，是用一种叫 Guesde 或名 Pastel 的草来染发的。

(301)指建立在马尔斯场的一个寺院。

(302)Ino，阿达马思 Athamas 后妻。她想将阿达马思前妻奈弗莱的子女弗里若克思 Phrixus 和海莱 Helle 弄死。但谋尔古虑思给了奈弗莱一头金毛的公羊，她把自己的子女放在羊背上，便从伊诺的手中脱逃出来，但海莱不幸在途中坠入海中。

(303)见注(302)。

(304)这儿指一种名叫 Cumatile 的布，Cumatile 一字是从希腊文“海”字(Kuma)变化出来的。

(305)指奥洛拉 Aurora，黎明女神。

(306)见注(195)。

(307)指昂德萝美黛。见注(18)。

(308)Seriphos，爱琴海中的一个岛。

(309)指奥维德所作 *Medicamina faciei feminae*。

(310)Myron，希腊著名雕刻家。

(311)指“出水的维纳斯”。

(312)罗马女子所崇拜的司生殖的女神，她的神祠是禁止男子入内的。

(313)罗马人的世仇。

(314)Semela，一位地上的女神，为裘比德所爱，和他生了巴古斯。

(315)Leda，斯巴达王登达勒思 Tyndareus 之妻，裘比德爱上了她，变成一头白鹅去亲近她，和她生了 Castor、Pollux、Clytemnestra、Helena。

(316)指欧罗巴[见注(71)]，因为她是福艾尼开的国王的女儿，而西同 Sidon 是福艾尼开的最古的城。

(317)指鳄鱼,妇女从它的腹中取出白色油脂来涂面。

(318)Umbrian,意大利的一个民族。

(319)Siren,是一种鸟形生着妇人头的海上怪物,唱着迷人的歌,使水手罹难。

(320)指屋里赛思,他的母亲曾被西昔福斯 Sisyphus 强暴。

(321)Rhodope,脱拉岂阿的山名。

(322)Orpheus,神话中脱拉岂阿的一个著名的游吟诗人。

(323) 指盎非雍 Amphion, 他的母亲盎蒂奥泊 Antiope 被他的叔父利古思 Lycus——带白的篡位王,及其妻子第尔凯 Dirce 所虐待,最后被害死。后来盎菲雍带领随从攻陷带白城,为母复仇。盎非雍擅长奏琴,演奏时能使石子自己聚拢起来,围成一座墙,以守卫领土。

(324)Arion,约公元前 7 世纪希腊 Lesbos 诗人,是一个著名的弹琴人。传说他航海被劫,又被投入海中,一只他用音乐引近船头的海豚救了他,并带他到了带纳鲁斯 Tacnarus。

(325)Callimachus,纪远前 4 世纪的希腊诗人。

(326)指 Philetas,Cos 人,为希腊诗人代奥克里都思 Theocritus 的老师。

(327)指阿纳克莱盎 Anacreon(纪元前 560~478 年),希腊诗人,生于 Teos。

(328)Sappho,希腊女诗人。

(329)指希腊人梅囊代尔 Menander。

(330)Propertius,纪元前 1 世纪罗马诗人。

(331)Gallus(纪元前 69~26 年),罗马诗人及雄辩家。

(332)Tibullus,罗马诗人,生于纪元前 54 年,死于纪元前 19 年(?)。

(333)Varro(纪元前 116~27 年),罗马诗人、杂文作家。

(334)见注(302)。

(335)指维尔吉留思 Vergilius 及其名作 *Aeneis*。

(336)Lethe,是冥土中的一条河,饮用它的水就会忘记过去的一切。“被莱带河的水所淹没”大约是被人遗忘了的意思。

(337)即指《爱的艺术》。

(338)指九位文艺女神。

(339)这种赌博称为:Ludus duodecim scriptorum。

(340)和前面所说的赌博不同,这是用十五只棋子的。

(341)Apua Virgo,在罗马体育场中,赛车或力量大的人,都去那里洗去灰尘和汗水。那里的泉水非常冷。

(342)指谛勃里斯河 Thybris。

(343)八月。

(344)见注(26)。

(345)Paraetonium,埃及沿海的一个城。此处指阿克沁战役 Actium(公元 31 年)。在那场战役中奥格斯特打败了安东尼和格莱奥芭特尔。

(346)“大帝”指奥古斯特,他的妹妹是屋大薇,他的王后是丽薇雅。他的女婿是马尔古斯·阿格里巴 Marcus Agrippa,他战胜安东尼的兵舰和塞克斯图斯·庞培 Sextus Pompeius。

(347)指伊西丝[见注(33)]。曼非斯 Memphis 是埃及名城。

(348)指巴尔步斯剧场、马尔凯卢斯剧场和庞培剧场。

(349)Thamyras,传说脱拉岂阿的一个诗人。

(350)Amoebeus,未详。

(351)Apelles,据奥维德称,他是生于高司岛的。他画了那幅名画“出水的维纳斯”,奥古斯特将这幅画藏在恺撒的庙堂里。日久画毁,奈罗 Nero 王代之以道罗德里 Dorotheus 所作“维纳斯像”。其时阿贝莱思重为高司岛人绘维纳斯像,较以前的作品更胜十倍,但是未完成阿贝莱思就死了。

(352)Scipio,罗马大将。

(353)Ennius,罗马大诗人,罗马史诗的创制者,于纪元前 239 年生于加拉勃里阿半岛 Calabria 之路第艾 Rudiae,没于纪元前 169 年。

(354)Danae,阿克思修思 Acrisius 之女。阿克思修思将她幽闭在塔中,裘比德变成金雨,冲破了她的塔得到了她,于是生了拜尔塞斯。

(355)指鹰。

(356)见注(18)。

(357)指珈桑特拉 Cassandra。

(358)见注(34)。

(359)指雅典女子,见注(39)。

(360)见注(201)。

(361)Vesta,罗马家神。

(362)Inachus,伊沃的父亲。

(363)Etna,意大利火山,传说是裘比德的雷电工场。

(364)见注(199)。

(365)笛子是葩拉丝 Pallas 发明的,但是当她在水中照见了自己吹笛时缩着嘴唇的样子,她便立刻把笛子丢了。奥维德在他的 Fastes 中有更有趣的叙述。

(366)Nemesis,谛蒲路思[见注(332)]诗中所歌咏的人。

(367)Cynthia,泊洛拜尔谛乌思[见注(330)]诗中所歌咏的人。

(368)Lycoris,加鲁思[见注(331)]诗中所歌咏的人。

(369)Corinna,奥维德诗中所歌咏的人,见所作《爱情》。

(370)这是一语双关的句子。

(371)因为缪赛们的居处海里公山 Helicon 是在鲍艾沃帝阿。

(372)指女子。

(373)Thais,雅典著名艺妓。

(374)这是罗马解放奴隶时代的仪式。

(375)Argus,有一百双眼睛,是裘娜派去监视伊沃的。

(376)Acrisius,阿尔哥斯 Argos 的国王,他的女儿是达纳爱,和裘比德生下拜尔塞斯。见注(354)。

(377)见注(312)。

(378)Adultera,是一把可以复制的钥匙的名称。奥维德的意思是说人们可以配一把和情妇家里的完全相同的钥匙。即使门已下锁,也可以打开门,进去和情妇幽会。

(379)指酒,黎阿谒士 Lyaeus 是酒神巴古斯的别名。

(380)见注(336)。

(381)见第二卷。

(382)见本章前面。

(383)泛指一般的女子。兰诺司 Lemmos 是爱琴海中的一个岛。岛上的女子,有一夜把所有的男子都杀害了,连自己的丈夫也不能幸免于难。

(384)Peocris,爱莱海得士 Erechtheus 之女。

(385)Hymettus,在阿非利加的一座山。

(386)见注(288)。

(387)指木瓜。启道奈阿 Cydonea 是一座在克莱特 Crete 北海岸上的古城。

(388)指谋尔古虑思 Mercurius,凯发路思的父亲,生在阿尔迦第阿 Arcadia 的岂莱耐山 Cyllene,又在那里长大。

(389)在那个时候人们还不用刀和叉。

(390)指巴黎斯。

(391)维纳斯之母,此处指维纳斯。

(392)Lucina,司生育的女神,是裘娜或第阿娜的别名。

(393)指盎特罗玛黑,见注(245)。她生在米西阿的带白。

(394)是一种三只脚的椅子,在那上面,代尔非 Eelphi 的女巫(Pythia)启示神意。

(395)Ammon,一个利比阿 Libya 的神祇,在罗马为人所供奉,称为裘比德阿孟 Jupiter Ammon。

(396)在诗歌里,维纳斯常常被描述为坐在天鹅驾着的车上。我们这位恋爱大诗人奥维德是很有资格坐在维纳斯女神身旁的。

图书在版编目（CIP）数据

爱的艺术 /（古罗马）奥维德著；戴望舒译 .-- 北京：北京联合出版公司，2014.10（2026.1 重印）

ISBN 978-7-5502-3298-3

Ⅰ.①爱… Ⅱ.①奥… ②戴… Ⅲ.①爱情－通俗读物 Ⅳ.① C913.1-49

中国版本图书馆 CIP 数据核字 (2014) 第 158798 号

爱的艺术

作　　者：［古罗马］奥维德

出 品 人：赵红仕

责任编辑：王　巍　陈　昊

封面设计：王　鑫

北京联合出版公司出版

（北京市西城区德外大街83号楼9层 100088）

北京新华先锋出版科技有限公司发行

北京雁林吉兆印刷有限公司印刷　新华书店经销

字数174千字　787毫米×1092毫米　1/16　13印张

2014年10月第1版　2026年1月第5次印刷

ISBN 978-7-5502-3298-3

定价：29.80元